Fearless Cooking for Men

Michele Evans

drawings, bill goldsmith

WARNER BOOKS

A Warner Communications Company

WARNER BOOKS EDITION

Copyright © 1977 Michele Evans
All rights reserved under International and Pan-American Copyright Conven-
tion. No part of this publication may be reproduced, stored in a retrieval system,
or transmitted, in any form, or by any means, electronic, mechanical, photo-
copying, recording or otherwise, without the prior permission of the publisher.

Library of Congress Catalog Card Number 77-22653

ISBN 0-446-72966-3

This Warner Books Edition is published by arrangement with Mason/Charter
Publishers, Inc.

Cover art by Gene Laurent

Warner Books, Inc., 75 Rockefeller Plaza, New York, N.Y. 10019

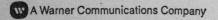 A Warner Communications Company

Printed in the United States of America

Not associated with Warner Press, Inc. of Anderson, Indiana

First Printing: December, 1978

10 9 8 7 6 5 4 3 2 1

FEARLESS COOKING FOR MEN

"*Everything* you always wanted to make but were afraid to try." —PLAYBOY Magazine

"Provides the *courage,* the *motivation* and *positive* attitude to get every man off the living room couch and into the kitchen." —*Baltimore News American*

"*Encouragingly* small, attractively illustrated... brief but clear...*comforting.*" —*New York Times Book Review*

"A *feast of fabulous meals* for the bachelor who lacks confidence in the kitchen." —King Features Syndicate

"Dedicated to the premise that food preparation can be *rewarding and easy,* this cookbook is chock-full of *imaginative* recipes and useful hints on food storage, kitchen supplies and cooking equipment... *straightforward* instructions and chatty anecdotes...handsomely illustrated." —*Library Journal*

"*Demystifies cooking* for anyone—male or female." —NEA

"A *fun, worthwhile* cookbook...cosmopolitan and sophisticated." —*Chicago Tribune*

"When it comes to gourmet cooking, most men are chicken. *Fearless Cooking for Men* will give new courage to even the most timid." —Frank Perdue

"It is just the gift for about-to-be-liberated men and would do very nicely too, as a hint to female cooks who have thought, all these years, that doing tuna/noodle with broken potato chips on top is really doing something." —*Detroit Free Press*

Books by
Michele Evans

The Slowcrock Cookbook
American Cuisine Minceur Cookbook
Fearless Cooking for Men

Published by
WARNER BOOKS

For Tully

contents

acknowledgements

I am indebted to the following men and women who contributed recipes, anecdotes, insights, dinner parties, good food, time and enthusiastic help in putting together this book in a spirit which reveals how much food means to all of us:

Helen and Jack Abbott, Bill Aller, Ken Auletta, Russell Banks, Mayor Abraham Beame, Bill Beutel, George Balasses, Leo Bloom, Robert Bunim, William E. Burrows, Ed Cohen, Dr. Lawrence S. Cohen, Judge Vincent Commisoa, Helen and Bob Davis, Mary Jo and Charles Dobson, Alfred Drake, John Drucker, Nancy Dussault, John Ehle, Maurice Evans, Clay Felker, Pat Fox, Bruce Jay Friedman, Sam Gallu, Paul, Zelda and John Gitlin, Sheila and Bobby Ginsberg, Milton Glaser, Bernard Grebanier, Henry Grossman, Jack Harrold, David Hartman, Arthur Herzog, Geoffrey Holder, Charles Hollerith, Jr., Anne Jeffreys, Edward Kleban, Paul Kovi, Daniel Labeille, David Liederman, Suzanne and Richard Levi, Joyce and Winfield Levi, Chef Ah-Yee Ma, Dr. Bruce McClennan, Bill Murfin, George Nelson, Ben Pagliaroli, Marvin Paige, Betty and Christopher Pappas, Jacques Pépin, Tully Plesser, Martin Pollner, Martin Rapp, Richard Reeves, Thomas Richmond, Harry Rigby, Harold Robbins, Jody Rodriguez, Audrey Roos, Steve Sohmer, André Soltner, Steven Thurston, Marvin Traub, Senator Lowell Weicker, Mayor Kevin H. White, Mr. X. and Jack Yogman.

Special thanks go to my patient friend and editor, Maureen Baron, for her unfailing support and encouragement.

foreword

At a dinner party one evening, I was seated next to a man whose obvious enjoyment of the meal was a pleasure to observe. He savored his food more than anyone I could recall, and he complimented the hostess several times on each dish. I was sure that anyone who loved food as much as he did would be a terrific cook. And when I asked him if he cooked, he replied, "Of course." A friend sitting across the table told me to ask the man his favorite recipe. I did.

My food-loving table companion said, "I make the world's best coffee. You take three eggs, a chopped tomato, a soupçon of garlic and pour boiling water over it." When the laughter died down, he admitted that he'd love to know how to cook, but he'd just never taken the time to learn and how could he possibly learn now?

The four men and four women who sat at the table began to discuss the question of cooking: Was it something women were born knowing? Who made the best cooks? The great chefs were usually men, how did they begin? The men seemed to be rather sure that if they set their minds to it they could conquer the mysteries of the kitchen. So, one of the women turned to her partner and asked if he knew the difference between frying and sauteing. Suddenly, the conversation turned into a game in which the men and women took turns asking and defining cooking terms. What did steep mean? Did one cup of chopped nuts mean the same as one cup of nuts, chopped? Which was more, three teaspoons or a tablespoon? And so forth.

The men scored badly, which they took badly. Playful and determined, however, they challenged the women to a return match at a dinner party to take place a month later. Secretaries were sent scurrying in search of various famous food sources: *Larousse Gastronomique, Escoffier's Cookbook, The Joy of Cooking,* etc. Waiters and butchers were interrogated and unsuspecting colleagues were showered with culinary information. "Never mind the stock market, let me tell you how to make a béchamel . . ."

One couple had a baby girl during the "campaign," and the first gift the baby received from her daddy was a tiny wire whisk.

When we readjourned to dine and play the game again, the men won hands down. They had all previously been non-cooks, but once their interest was aroused, there was no stopping them. They couldn't let all that fascinating information go to waste—trying it out was the next step.

And that's how *Fearless Cooking For Men* was born. I was convinced that men could learn to cook, easily and eagerly, if they were provided with a little basic information, clear instructions and interesting recipes.

Until recently few men cooked at home. Today, with more women working and enjoying careers, it is essential to family happiness for men to be able to help out around the house. Cooking is certainly one of the more satisfying chores, and I would hope to many, a pure pleasure.

Whether a man has a family or is a bachelor, whether he is eating alone or entertaining guests, if he knows how to cook, he is really ahead of the game. Naturally, this book will work equally as well for women, but I have written it to encourage men who hesitate to venture into the kitchen, much in the same spirit as one might write a book on carpentry for women who are skeptical of their talents in the workshop.

Jacques Pépin, a French chef and teacher, insists that teaching beginners is the easiest, because the student who knows nothing about cooking does not have to rid himself of the rigid and often unnecessary rules that other students have somehow acquired. So, this book is for those men who are afraid cooking is a mysterious process that takes too much time and trouble to master. I've tried to give simple and basic explanations and directions in cooking terms, procedures, measurements and actual recipes.

Of course, you learn to cook by experience as much as by anything else. If you burn the butter once, you'll learn to keep the heat lower, and you'll learn that butter won't burn as easily if you *clarify* it first. Now don't back away. Just check the glossary to learn how to clarify butter. Once you've gained a few such skills you will find yourself proceeding fearlessly, as promised, into the wonderful world of cooking.

Good luck and happy cooking.

Michele Evans.

Collecting stories, recipes and ultimate meals from many men friends who rate gastronomic pleasure high on life's list of priorities has been a joy and education for me. All men generously shared their philosophies and experiences of cooking and food with good humor and fervor. They were more than eager to contribute their culinary wisdom in the pursuit of greater satisfaction in the kitchen for men everywhere.

He may live without books,
  What is knowledge but grieving?
He may live without hope,
  What is hope but deceiving?
He may live without love,
  What is passion but pining?
But where is a man that can
  live without dining?

OWEN MEREDITH, *Lucile*

introduction

A FEW RULES TO REMEMBER

As the famous chef Fernand Point said, "In cooking, one is a student all one's life." Even when you've mastered a dish and repeat it regularly, it will differ slightly each time depending on ingredients, cooking temperature and even weather. For example, preparing pie dough is more difficult on a hot day because the shortening melts so easily. The dough has to be refrigerated before it can be rolled out successfully. Marble is often used as a surface for rolling dough because it's cool. But on a hot day, even marble will not be cool enough. Once you've learned and applied such points of information, the execution of any dish will be a triumph instead of a disaster.

Part of being fearless is the ability to predict what will happen, and, in cooking, knowing a few essentials will enable you to proceed unafraid.

Here are several general rules to follow as you try a recipe. They are basics for general cooking at all levels.

1. Read each recipe through before beginning to cook, so you'll be able to assemble ingredients, cooking utensils, pots and pans and know if you need to have the oven preheated before a dish goes in the oven.

2. Use exact amounts given in recipes. If you fancy wine and a recipe calls for ¼ cup, don't use ½ cup or the recipe will be overwhelmed with the flavor of wine and will contain too much liquid.

3. Cook in proper size pots, pans and baking dishes. Boiling a pound of spaghetti in a 2-quart saucepan will certainly cause it to stick together and turn out pasty. Use a large pot with 6 to 8 quarts of water so the pasta can move freely, cook evenly and be cleansed in an abundance of water. When roasting a small chicken, don't use a large roasting pan or the basting and bird

juices will be spread too thinly over the bottom of the pan, and will burn.

4. When sauteeing anything in butter, don't melt the butter over high heat. The butter will burn before you can say Auguste Escoffier. Low heat and a tablespoon or two of oil added to the butter will prevent the butter from burning so easily. As I said in the foreword, clarified butter won't burn as quickly either. Check index for instructions on preparation of clarified butter.

5. Don't oversalt food while cooking. Use amount stated in recipes and check flavor near the end of cooking time. Nothing will spoil a dish faster than saltiness. Wine intensifies the flavor of salt, so use salt sparingly in a dish that contains wine.

6. Generally speaking, don't boil foods, unless it is specifically required by the recipe. Directions in recipes will often read "bring to a boil, reduce heat and simmer." Boiling will rob foods of nutrients and flavor.

7. Don't overcook foods. The result will be soggy and tasteless. A fresh, beautiful asparagus will wilt and be ruined if overcooked. To prevent overcooking follow recipe's specified cooking time and test carefully. You can always cook a dish longer if you feel it needs more, but there's no way to undo the overdone.

8. Let roasts, cakes and breads rest before carving or cutting, or they will be stringy and crumble.

9. Follow directions about size and shape of foods in a recipe. If a recipe calls for minced onions, don't take less time and chop the onions too coarse. It takes longer to cook larger pieces of onions and the dish might come out unevenly cooked. Of course, certain instructions about slicing or chopping a particular ingredient may be entirely for aesthetic purposes, but they should still be followed to insure that the dish will turn out as planned.

10. When sauteeing or frying, let the shortening get hot before adding ingredients or the food will absorb the fat. However, don't let the fat burn or smoke.

11. Be careful not to make substitutions unless your common sense tells you it will be all right. Canned, but drained, tomatoes

can be substituted for fresh tomatoes in most cooked dishes. Not in salads. A friend who was making Beef Stroganoff couldn't find any fresh mushrooms, so he added a can of cream of mushroom soup. That may be an outrageous example, but it happened. Tomato juice can't be substituted for tomato sauce, although scallions can generally take the place of shallots.

12. When using dried herbs, remember that drying makes them stronger in flavor. If a recipe calls for 1 tablespoon of chopped fresh basil, use only ½ teaspoon of dried basil.

13. In most cases you do not add an ingredient to a pan or pot or baking dish that is to be put directly over heat or in the oven without shortening covering the bottom lightly, unless the dish is being cooked in liquid. The shortening prevents sticking.

14. Timing is very important when planning a meal. Work out your timing of each dish so that they will all be hot when served. I call this orchestration. Check the cooking time for each recipe and cook them in order.

15. Try to vary the way different dishes in a meal are cooked. In other words, don't bake everything you're cooking. Not only is it unlikely that it would all fit in the oven, but the probability that all the dishes would require the same cooking temperature is low. Bake a vegetable, saute the meat and prepare a salad. If the dessert is to be baked, prepare it early in the day, etc.

16. Presentation of a dish is always important. An attractively arranged fish dish garnished with parsley and lemon wedges (no seeds) will enhance its appeal. Simple food garnishes are best, unless it is a spectacular dish and you're willing to go to the trouble to make a ship of toasted bread sails or spin sugar into bows to attach to a basket.

17. Part of presentation is color. The dishes served should vary in color. Don't give your guests the white treatment: poached fish, rice and a glass of milk.

18. Finally, arrange your table attractively. One little flower in a bud vase will do wonders for a table setting. Always use napkins, and some kind of cloth or mat.

FOOD STORAGE

Books have been written on the proper way to store food, but there are a few basic suggestions that will help you maintain the quality of your food and at the same time make it last longer.

Potatoes and Onions:

The best way to store these two important staples of cooking is to place each in a shallow wicker basket so that the air will circulate around them. Sometimes they come packaged in plastic bags with tiny air holes. Immediately remove the bag and place them in a basket. Buy only the amount you are likely to be using in the next week or two because they will soften and sprout.

Leftovers:

When storing any food in the refrigerator as a leftover, be sure to wrap it up tightly in foil, plastic wrap or a jar. If the food must go in a bowl, cover the top tightly. This will protect the food and also keep the aroma of the food out of other articles of food in the refrigerator.

Butter or Margarine:

Nothing absorbs other flavors as fast as butter or margarine. Be sure to wrap it up carefully. If you have several pounds on hand, it can be frozen.

Herbs and Spices:

Dried herbs and spices should be kept in dry, dark places with the lids of the jars tightly closed. They will keep for 6 months well cared for. However, after 6 months their strength and color will fade.

Chicken and Turkey:

If you have roast chicken or turkey leftovers, remove the meat from the carcass and wrap it tightly in plastic wrap and foil. This will prevent the meat from drying out, and you'll also use less space storing it in the refrigerator. The carcass, with the addition of water, vegetables and herbs, makes a good stock.

IMPORTANT COOKING TERMS

There are many special terms used in cookbooks and, though most of them will be familiar to you, some you may be unsure of, and others you will not know at all. In order to be a successful cook, it is important to understand exactly what the words in a recipe mean. A few of the terms are self-explanatory; for example, to brush something means to apply an ingredient such as butter or egg yolk to another food with a pastry brush. Other terms must be learned. In cooking, for instance, to score something has nothing to do with the playing field. It means to make shallow slits or gashes with a knife or fork in the outer surface of the food.

When you first look over a recipe, if there are any new or unfamiliar terms in it, refer to this glossary to learn exactly what is to be done, *before you begin to prepare the dish.*

I've included the most essential terms and have tried to keep the explanations short and to the point so that you can learn what you need to know quickly and proceed to the cooking well advised.

GLOSSARY

Al Dente—An Italian phrase which means "to the tooth." This term is used to describe pasta which is cooked only to the point of offering the slightest resistance when bitten into.

Aspic—A jelly-like substance made with the juices of meat or vegetables with gelatin added, then chilled.

Au Gratin—Cooked with either crumbs or grated cheese (or both) on top of the dish, the top then browned in the oven or under a broiler.

Au Jus—Served with natural juices or gravy, often of beef.

Bake—To cook in oven by dry steady heat. Cooking meat by this method is called roasting.

Baste—With a large spoon or pastry brush, moisten food with liquid such as sauce, marinade, butter or oil during cooking in order to prevent drying out or burning and to add flavor.

Batter—A slightly thickened liquid mixture, such as crepe batter, that can be poured.

Beat—To mix by rapidly stirring by hand or electric mixer.

Blanch—To cook a food briefly in boiling water, to remove excess fat in the case of bacon, or loosen skin from such foods as tomatoes or nuts.

Blend—To combine ingredients evenly, usually with a spoon, in a circular motion.

Boil—To cook liquid until bubbles break on the surface. Water boils at 212 F. at sea level.

Bouquet Garni—Herbs in a little bag made of cheesecloth. The bag is used to add flavoring to a dish while it's cooking and is discarded when done.

Braise—To brown in small amount of fat, then cook slowly in a small amount of liquid in a covered pan.

Bread—To coat food with dried bread crumbs in order to form crisp crust on food which is to be baked or fried.

Broil—To cook under or over direct heat.

Brown—To cook food until it actually turns brown in color either by cooking it in the oven, under a broiler or on top of a stove in a pan with a little fat. Browning meat seals in the flavor and makes it appealing to the eye.

Brush—To coat food with fat, egg, or liquid with pastry brush.

Caramelize—To heat sugar until melted and browned or to coat food with sugar which has browned by this process.

Casserole—A deep, heavy dish with a tight-fitting lid, in which food is baked and served.

Chill—To cool food in refrigerator until cold, but not frozen.

Chop—To cut food into small pieces. Chopped food pieces are larger than minced food pieces.

Clarify—To clear greaseless stock by adding egg whites and shells and simmering for several minutes. The stock is then skimmed and strained. Butter can also be clarified by melting slowly over heat. Milk solids sink to bottom leaving clear yellow clarified butter. This liquid butter is poured off and used to cook with. Clarified butter burns less quickly than regular butter. It can be refrigerated in a jar with a tight-fitting lid for a few weeks.

Coat—To roll or sprinkle food with a layer of another food such as bread crumbs or mayonnaise.

Cream—To mix a single ingredient or more to a creamy consistency.

Crisp—To wash lettuce or other vegetable in cold water in order to firm it, or to cook in any manner until food is cooked but still crunchy.

Croutons—Small pieces of bread either fried or toasted until crisp.

Cube—To cut food into uniform cube shapes of small size.

Deep-Fry—To cook food totally immersed in hot fat.

Dice—To cut food into small cubes or squares. Diced food is smaller than cubed food.

Dissolve—To mix dry ingredient with liquid.

Dredge—To coat food with flour, corn meal, bread crumbs, sugar or other ingredient.

Drippings—The fat expelled from meat while roasting or frying.

Filet—A piece of meat or fish from which all the bones have been removed.

Flake—To break apart a food such as fish with the gentle use of a fork so that it resembles flakes.

Fold in—To blend one mixture with another with a spoon or spatula in a folding motion. The movement is from the bottom up and over ingredients and repeated.

Fry—To cook food in hot fat. Fried food can be cooked immersed in fat or only partly covered.·

Garnish—A decoration of some colorful food added to a prepared dish to enhance its appearance.

Glaze—To coat or cover food with a glossy coat called a glaze by covering it with icing, aspic, syrup or sauce.

Grate—To rub a food over a grater so that it is reduced to tiny particles or thin shreds.

Grease—To lightly coat a surface with butter or oil.

Grill—To cook under or over direct heat.

Grind—To reduce food to a powdery consistency such as coffee, pepper or flour, or pass through meat grinder.

Julienne—To cut food such as carrots, potatoes or cheese into thin, even strips.

Knead—To repeatedly press, pull and fold dough into smooth mass with hands on flat, lightly-floured surface.

Lard—To insert fat into flesh of meat with special needle to make meat juicier.

Legumes—Vegetables, including beans, peas and lentils; French.

Marinate—To allow a food to rest in a mixture to season and sometimes tenderize it.

Melt—To heat butter or other food and reduce to liquid state.

Mince—To cut pieces of food into very small bits.

Pan-broil—To cook in uncovered skillet over direct heat.

Pan-fry—To cook in small amount of fat in skillet.

Parboil—Boiling a food until partially cooked. Cooking is then completed by some other method.

Pare—To peel outer skin with peeler or sharp knife.

Peel—To remove outer skin or layer of a food by using sharp knife. Thin-skinned fruit or vegetables, such as peaches or tomatoes, may be immersed in boiling water for 8 seconds and skins will easily be removed with the help of a small pointed knife.

Pinch—Approximately $1/8$ of a teaspoon. Usually referring to salt, sugar, nutmeg, etc. Something that can be held between the forefinger and thumb.

Pit—To remove seed from food.

Poach—To simmer food gently in hot liquid.

Preheat—To allow oven or pan to reach exact temperature required to cook dish before putting it in the oven.

Puree—To reduce food to a smooth mixture by use of a sieve, food mill, electric blender or food processor.

Reduce—To evaporate some of liquid by boiling.

Render—To melt solid fat, usually animal fat, such as chicken fat, lard or suet, by cooking slowly. Also called "to try out."

Roast—To cook food (especially meat) by dry heat in oven or on a spit over heat.

Saute—To cook a food in a small amount of fat over direct heat in skillet or other pan.

Scald—To heat liquid to the point just before it boils.

Scallop—Layers of food baked with or without sauce in casserole, usually covered with bread crumbs. Also thinly sliced meat, such as veal.

Score—To make shallow slits or gashes with knife or fork through outer surface of a food (usually fat of roast, etc.)

Sear—To brown meat quickly in a pan over intense heat.

Season—To add flavor to a food by the addition of salt, pepper or other seasoning, herb or spice.

Shred—To tear or cut food into thin strips or pieces.

Shuck—To remove covering of food such as the husk of corn or shells of clams or oysters.

Sift—To put dry ingredients through fine sieve.

Simmer—To cook food gently in liquid just below boiling point.

Skewer—A thin metal or wooden pin on which food is secured and cooked.

Skim—To remove fat or particles from surface of a liquid with spoon, ladle or skimmer (shallow, perforated disk with long handle). To remove cream from milk.

Sliver—A thin shred of food.

Sponge—A batter made from yeast.

Steam—To cook food by direct steam on a rack placed in deep container holding small amount of boiling water.

Steep—To let substance such as tea stand in a liquid, usually hot water.

Stir—To mix 2 or more ingredients in circular motion with spoon.

Stock—A liquid in which food has cooked.

Tenderize—To soften tough fibers of meat by pounding with implement resembling a gavel designed for this purpose. Meat can also be tenderized by marination.

Terrine—A baking dish with lid for making pâtés. Usually made of earthenware.

Thicken—To make substance (usually a sauce) become thick by the use of thickening agents such as arrowroot, cornstarch or eggs, or by cooking food longer to cause evaporation and therefore thickening a sauce or gravy.

Toast—To brown or make crisp.

Truss—To secure legs and wings of poultry or game with a string so meat will cook more evenly.

Try out—To melt animal fat. Also called render.

Whip—To beat mixture by hand with whisk or electric beater, incorporating air into mixture and increasing its volume.

MEASUREMENTS

Correct measurements are as basic and necessary to good cooking
as quality ingredients are. Fortunately, there are only a few measurements you will need to learn for cooking. The ones listed
below are actually liquid measurements, but they also apply to dry
ingredients in this cookbook, as in most others. Pints and quarts
are used only for fluids. You will need 2 types of measuring
cups—dry and liquid. One set of 4 dry measuring cups consisting
of ¼-cup, ⅓-cup, ½-cup and 1-cup. These cups are used to measure exactly a dry ingredient, such as flour or sugar, by filling the
cup to the top and then smoothing top of ingredient over cup with
the back of a knife. The liquid cup, which should be a 2-cup size,
looks like a pitcher and enables you to pour the required liquid
amount in to the proper measuring mark but will still leave room
at the top to prevent spillage. You will also need to own a set of
measuring spoons containing ¼-teaspoon, ½-teaspoon, 1-
teaspoon and 1-tablespoon.

1 teaspoon	equals	⅓ tablespoon
1 tablespoon	equals	3 teaspoons
4 tablespoons	equals	¼ cup
1 fluid ounce	equals	2 tablespoons
1 cup	equals	½ pint or 8 fluid ounces
2 cups	equals	1 pint
1 quart	equals	2 pints
1 gallon	equals	4 quarts

For this cookbook you won't need to learn that 8 quarts of dry
ingredients equal 1 peck or that 4 pecks equal 1 bushel.

METRIC EQUIVALENTS

¼ teaspoon (t)	1.5 ml	1 pint	600 ml
½ t	3 ml	2 pints	1.25 litre
1 t	5 ml	3 pints	1.90 litre
2 t	10 ml	4 pints	2.5 litre
3 t	15 ml		
4 t	20 ml	1 oz	30 g
		2 oz	60 g
1 Tablespoon (T)	12.5 ml	4 oz	125 g
2 T	25 ml	8 oz	250 g
3 T	37.5 ml		
4 T	50 ml	1 lb	500 g
		2 lb	1 kg
¼ cup (c)	60 ml	3 lb	1.5 kg
⅓ c	80 ml	4 lb	2 kg
½ c	125 ml	5 lb	2.5 kg
¾ c	190 ml		
1 c	250 ml		
2 c	500 ml		
3 c	750 ml		
4 c	1 litre		

OVEN TEMPERATURES

C	F	C	F
100	200	200	400
120	250	220	425
140	275	240	475
160	325	260	500
180	350	280	550

OVEN TEMPERATURE CHART

very slow oven	250 F.	moderately hot	375 F.
slow oven	300 F.	hot	400 F.
moderate slow oven	325 F.	very hot	450 to 500 F.
moderate oven	350 F.	broil	500 and over

SO YOUR CUPBOARD SHOULDN'T BE BARE

Cupboards in bachelor quarters often hold only dishes and salt and pepper, and refrigerators contain a few bottles of beer and a wilted lemon wedge. All this will change, of course, once you really get into cooking. But there are a few items you should always keep on hand, so that you'll be in business whether you're snowed in, hiding out, guests drop by or you're just cooking for yourself. Once you have them, simply replace as used.

Herbs and Spices

basil	cumin	paprika
bay leaves	curry powder	peppercorns
bouquet garni	garlic powder	rosemary
celery seeds	onion powder	seasoned salt
chili powder	oregano	salt
chives	nutmeg	tarragon
cinnamon	parsley flakes	thyme

An Important Message About Pepper

Freshly ground pepper is essential to good cooking. Pre-ground, powdery, pre-packaged pepper quickly loses its strength and flavor. The implement for grinding peppercorns is a peppermill. It comes in a variety of materials, shapes and sizes. So, you can be thrifty or extravagant when buying one, but it is a basic necessity for table and kitchen.

A small electric coffee grinder can also be used to grind peppercorns and any other spice.

Other Useful Items

anchovies	clams (chopped, canned)
baking powder	coffee
baking soda	cornstarch
beef bouillon cubes	eggs
bread crumbs	flour
butter (or margarine)	garlic
chicken bouillon cubes	granulated sugar

lemons
milk
onions
Parmesan cheese (grated)
pasta
potatoes
rice
sardines
soy sauce
sugar

Tabasco
tea or tea bags
tomatoes (whole canned)
tomato paste
tomato sauce
tunafish (white meat)
vegetable oil
wine vinegar
Worcestershire sauce

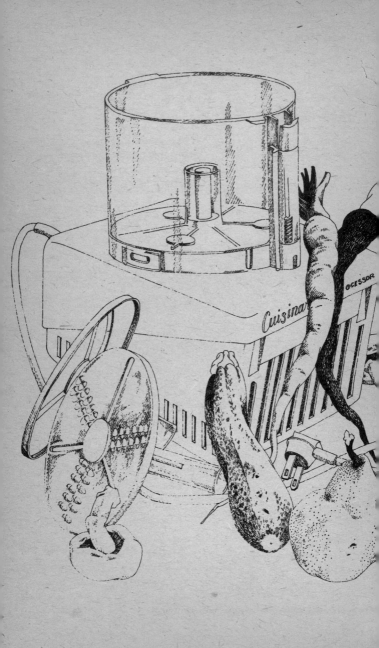

Chapter 1.

experimenting with
the Cuisinart® food processor
crepe pan
clay pot
slow crock cooker
wok
microwave oven

Collecting cooking equipment and utensils is a great hobby. I love to browse in the kitchenware section of department stores and in specialty kitchen equipment shops. When you travel, it is a pleasant way to make yourself feel at home in any country. I cherish the ceramic olive oil pitcher I bought in Italy and my set of egg coddlers from England. If you find yourself in Paris, don't miss the experience of E. Dehillerin.* It is probably the most famous and well-equipped culinary equipment shop in the world. However, while it is fun to build your kitchen collection with specialty items such as a croissant cutter or a leg of lamb holder, only a small amount of equipment is actually needed to enable you to cook well.

Pots and pans and good sharp knives are at the top of the list of essentials, but you'll need a measuring cup and potato peeler, too. The list that follows was compiled to help you meet the immediate needs for cooking almost anything. You can always improvise—use a strainer instead of a colander, for instance—but for comfort and best results you will need most of the items below.

Small Implements

balloon whisk
bottle opener
can opener
corkscrew
food grater
kitchen string
ladle
measuring spoons
mouli grater
pastry brush

potato masher
rolling pin
salad knife and fork
set of 4 dry measuring
  cups
slotted spoon
spatula
strainer (small and
  medium size)
tenderizer gavel

tongs
trussing needle
2-cup liquid
  measuring cup
vegetable peeler
wire whisk
  (8-inch)
wooden spoon

Miscellaneous

cannister set
chopping block, small for onions and garlic, etc.; large butcher
  block for meats and vegetables
fruit juicer
set of mixing bowls
teakettle

*The address of E. Dehillerin is 18, Rue Coquillière, Paris 75001.

Knives

small, sharp paring knife
7-inch cutting knife
10-inch chopping knife
14-inch carving knife

chef's fork
steel to sharpen knives
clam knife
oyster knife

Pots and Pans

1½-quart saucepan with cover
3½-quart saucepan with cover
5-quart Dutch oven or pot
  with cover
double boiler
8-inch skillet with curved sides
10-inch skillet with cover
14-inch skillet with cover
roasting pan, medium and large
2 shallow baking dishes
  (12-inch and 16-inch)

meat loaf pan
8-inch square cake pan
3 8- or 9-inch cake pans
pie plate or dish
baking sheet
2½-quart and 5½-quart
  casserole dishes with covers
6- to 8-quart crock dish
  with cover
6- to 8-quart pot with cover

Electric Equipment

electric can opener
electric blender (See notes that follow)
electric mixer
Cuisinart® food processor (See section on this miracle worker)
toaster

For Serving Your Meal

large glass pitcher
salad bowl
2 vegetable serving dishes
1 au gratin dish about 14-inches long
2 large oval serving dishes
large platter
sauce boat and spoon
salt and pepper mill

set of steak knives
trivets
butter dish
wine glasses
water goblets
cocktail glasses
large serving tray
bread basket

Notes on the Blender

The electric blender is an important machine to have in the kitchen. While the Cuisinart unit can accomplish many more chores such as mixing, shredding, slicing and grinding, the blender is still more efficient in blending liquids, sauces and pureeing for soup making.

Remember when using a blender to fill the container only half full and turn it on low for the first speed. Also place your hand on the lid to avoid splattering the kitchen walls and yourself.

An electric blender is excellent for mixing drinks such as Bloody Marys or Margaritas

Special cooking equipment

Most men who cook love kitchen gadgets and new equipment, which is great. The conservative cook misses a lot of special and wonderful implements. Not only that, I feel that any help one can get in the kitchen is worth investigating. I am all for experimenting with new ways of doing things, but add a cautionary word about fad items that promise miracles but don't deliver.

As in most things, there are fads in cooking equipment, too. Every year a new "marvel" comes along that the trend followers *must* have. Some are really new, others just rediscovered. I remember at one point, several years ago, no self-respecting host or hostess dared give a party without a pot of fondue bubbling away on the buffet. This year the crepe madness has hit. I love crepes, but I am not fond of the new crepe pans introduced to make them the latest craze—as I explain in the section on crepes that follows. Often, these gadgets are as useless as they are expensive and the uninitiated discover this fact only after their investment.

There are, however, five special cooking aids that I believe are really worth purchasing: the Cuisinart® food processor, the old-fashioned crepe pan used by the French, the clay pot, the slow crock cooker and the wok. I explain why and give sample recipes for each in the special section that follows. I have also included a brief discussion of the microwave oven at the end of this section since it is very much a part of the contemporary scene. It is not one of my favorite appliances, as you will see.

EXPERIMENTING WITH THE CUISINART® FOOD PROCESSOR

"The discovery of a new dish does more for the happiness of man than the discovery of a new star."

BRILLAT SAVARIN, *The Physiology of Taste*

"The invention of the Cuisinart® food processor does more for the happiness of man than the invention of the electric razor."

MICHELE EVANS

The most outstanding kitchen aid to come along in years is undoubtedly the Cuisinart food processor. Having a Cuisinart unit is the same as having an experienced assistant in the kitchen working with you. It slices, shreds, purees, blends, grinds and mixes superbly.

This food processor is manufactured in France and is distributed in the United States from Greenwich, Connecticut. It is expensive, but this sturdy multi-purpose machine is a wizard at saving time, and serious cooks should consider the expenditure as necessary. A Cuisinart food processor is to a cook what a typewriter is to a writer.

It consists of a clear plastic container mounted on a plastic base which holds the motor. Four attachments are used in the container: a two-bladed stainless steel knife, a two-bladed plastic knife, a stainless steel slicing disk and a shredding disk. The stainless steel knife is used for all blending or pureeing or grinding procedures. It also makes bread crumbs and chops nuts. I find the plastic knife unnecessary. The shredding disk is used to shred vegetables and the slicing disk slices potatoes, carrots, zucchini, cucumbers, etc. The lid of the container has a mouth through which foods can be pressed with a plastic pusher. Other attachments such as a fine-shredding disk and a fine-slicing disk can be obtained in specialty kitchen shops and department stores. The latest attachment available is a French-fry cutter. There are also special racks for holding the Cuisinart unit attachments.

There are only a few things the food processor can't do and those include whipping egg whites and uniformly chopping or dicing food. It has a powerful motor and, for safety's sake, the machine won't go on until the container is in place with the top on and it is turned on by a counter-clockwise motion of the hand. A booklet of instructions accompanying the Cuisinart unit shows how easy it is to work with this fantastic machine.

Some of my favorite recipes for this machine follow.

CARROTS VICHY

1 pound carrots, scraped and trimmed
3 tablespoons butter
¼ teaspoon salt
freshly ground pepper
¼ teaspoon sugar
¼ cup chicken broth
1 teaspoon freshly chopped parsley

Using the slicing blade of the Cuisinart food processor slice carrots by putting two or three carrots at a time through mouth of container. In a saucepan heat butter, salt, pepper, sugar and chicken broth. Bring to a boil and add carrots. Reduce heat to a simmer and cook about 10 minutes, covered. Shake pan occasionally to prevent burning. Sprinkle with parsley.

Serves 4.

HAM SOUFFLÉ

¾ pound boiled ham, coarsely chopped
4 tablespoons butter
3 egg yolks
½ pint heavy cream, whipped

Put steel knife in Cuisinart food processor. Place ham and butter in container and process for about 25 seconds until fairly smooth. Turn mixture into bowl. Add egg yolks and stir. Fold whipped cream into mixture. Put mixture into 1-quart mold, and place in baking pan or dish with water that reaches three quarters up the side of the mold. Bake in preheated 350 F. oven for about 45 minutes.

Serves 4 to 6 as appetizer.

CHOPPED STEAK

1 pound boneless round steak, cut into 1½-inch pieces
1 teaspoon Worcestershire sauce
2 tablespoons chopped onions
¼ teaspoon salt
freshly ground pepper to taste

Place several pieces of steak in Cuisinart food processor with stainless steel knife. Turn machine on for 5 seconds and add more meat until it is all ground. Scrape down sides of container with rubber spatula occasionally. Place ground beef in bowl with remaining ingredients and mix well. Shape into 4 ovals and broil 4 or 5 minutes on each side until desired doneness.

Serves 4.

TURKEY TONNATO

1 8-ounce can white meat tuna, drained
2 cloves garlic, crushed
1 cup mayonnaise
1 teaspoon lemon juice
8 anchovy filets, chopped
½ cup olive oil
4 tablespoons capers
1 breast of turkey, cooked and sliced thinly

Place stainless steel knife in food processor. Add tuna, garlic, mayonnaise, lemon juice and anchovy filets. Turn machine on and puree mixture until smooth. Next, pour olive oil through mouth of container until mixture is smooth while machine is on. Turn mixture into bowl and fold in 3 tablespoons of capers. Arrange sliced turkey on serving platter and spoon tuna sauce around border. Sprinkle dish with remaining capers and garnish with lemon wedges.

Serves 4.

CHICKEN CUTLETS POJARSKY

*4 medium-size chicken breasts, skinned, boned and cut
    into small pieces*
½ cup heavy cream
2 tablespoons vodka
5 slices fresh white bread, crusts trimmed off and discarded, cut into cubes
4 ounces sweet butter (or 1 stick), at room temperature
½ teaspoon salt
freshly grated nutmeg
flour
3 eggs, beaten
bread crumbs
3 tablespoons oil
3 tablespoons clarified butter (See glossary for method.)

Place steel blade in Cuisinart food processor and put pieces of chicken breasts in container. Process until chicken is well ground. Remove ground chicken meat to large bowl. Place heavy cream, vodka and bread cubes in another bowl. When bread has absorbed as much liquid as it can, squeeze out most of liquid. Place bread in bowl with chicken and add butter, salt and nutmeg. Mix well. Refrigerate this mixture for 30 minutes. Divide mixture into 12 parts. Form each section into the shape of a chop, about 1-inch thick and 3½-inches long. Coat lightly with flour. Dip in beaten egg and roll in bread crumbs. Saute in oil and butter mixture until golden brown on each side.

Serve with lemon wedges.
Serves 6.

CREPE PAN

Crepe cooking has made a comeback. Ten years ago, while touring with *Kismet* in Detroit, the company manager, Dick Grayson, held a crepe party after the show. He cooked the crepes and the cast selected the fillings. There were about thirty of us and he kept three crepe pans going for about an hour. We all ate more than we should have.

Crepes are elegant and delicious. They're easy to prepare, economical and, properly wrapped, can be stored in the refrigerator or freezer on top of each other until you're ready to use them. They are the latest cooking fad now, however, because an incredible number of newly designed crepe pans have recently appeared on the market. Over twenty-five at last count. There are upside down crepe pans, electric crepe pans, non-sticking crepe pans, crepe Suzette pans, omelet-type pans and others. Some of the new models work satisfactorily, but many do not. Some, like the upside-down pan, enable you to cook the crepe only on one side; the pan must be dipped into the crepe batter in a wide bowl—a method that wastes batter. Others run off the side of the pan until you get the knack of how to use just the right amount of batter at perfect consistency. Some produce rubbery crepes. I recommend the classic French crepe pans of steel. They work perfectly and are inexpensive. These pans are sold in department stores and specialty kitchen shops across the country. Crepe is a French word meaning "thin pancake," but many countries have their own version of "crepes": the Jewish blintz, the Mexican tortilla, the Italian cannelloni and the Chinese eggroll, to name a few.

Crepes are superb as a first course, entree or dessert, and guests are always impressed with them.

Recipes usually advise you to refrigerate the crepe batter ½ to 1 hour before making crepes to allow the flour to grow. I have watched a French chef whip up herb crepe batter and cook crepes immediately with beautiful results. However, for my favorite crepe recipes, I follow the old rule of letting the batter rest.

Directions for successful crepes are in the recipes that follow. I included recipes for basic crepe batter and for dessert batter. These will make crepes that can then be filled according to your own taste, but I'll get you started with a few suggestions.

BASIC CREPE BATTER

½ cup flour
¼ teaspoon salt
1 tablespoon vegetable oil
2 whole eggs
1 cup milk
¼ cup water

Combine flour, salt, oil and eggs. Beat in milk and water. Refrigerate for at least 30 minutes. Pour about ¼ cup of crepe batter into hot, well-oiled 7-inch crepe pan and tilt pan until batter covers pan. When crepe begins to bubble and brown at edges, turn over with spatula and cook for about 20 seconds. Place finished crepes on top of each other in plate. Crepes can be covered and refrigerated for a day or wrapped and frozen until ready to use.

CHEESE CREPES:

Add ¼ shredded Cheddar or Gruyère cheese to basic crepe mixture and cook crepes.

MORNAY SAUCE FILLING:

2 tablespoons butter
2 tablespoons flour
1 cup milk
salt and pepper
¼ cup shredded Gruyère cheese

Melt butter and stir in flour. Cook over medium heat for 1 minute. Slowly pour heated milk over flour mixture, whisking constantly. Season with salt and pepper and stir in cheese. Continue stirring with whisk until sauce reaches the boil and is thick and smooth. Spread crepes with sauce and roll up and place in buttered au gratin dish. Sprinkle with grated cheese and dot with butter. Place in 400 F. oven and cook for several minutes until crepes are golden and cheese has melted.

Garnish with fresh chopped parsley.

Serves 4 to 6.

Basic Crepe Suggestions:

RED CAVIAR AND SOUR CREAM:

Spoon two tablespoons of sour cream and 1 tablespoon of red caviar in center of each crepe. Roll up
and top with a dollop of sour cream and a little red
caviar.

SAUSAGE AND CHEDDAR CHEESE:

Crumble cooked sausage and spoon 2 tablespoons
in center of each crepe. Sprinkle with 1 tablespoon
of grated cheese. Roll up crepe. Place crepes side by
side in shallow baking dish and sprinkle with
grated cheese. Pass under the broiler until cheese
melts. Serve immediately.

BROCCOLI-FILLED CREPES:

Cook fresh or frozen broccoli spears. Drain. Place
two spears in each crepe and roll up. Top with Hollandaise Sauce. (or substitute 2 or 3 stalks cooked
asparagus in this recipe.)

HERB CREPES:

Add 1 teaspoon chopped fresh parsley and ½ teaspoon dried tarragon to basic crepe recipe.

Filling: Prepare 1½ cups béchamel sauce (see index
for recipe). Add 1 cup chopped ham. Spread filling
mixture over crepes and roll.

SPINACH CREPES:

Prepare 1½ cups béchamel sauce. Add 1 cup cooked
chopped spinach, which has been well drained, and
¼ cup shredded Cheddar cheese. Spread over basic
crepes and roll.

DESSERT CREPES:

1 cup flour
2 tablespoons sugar
pinch of salt
4 eggs
1 cup water
1 cup milk

Combine flour, sugar and salt and beat in eggs, water and milk with wire whisk until smooth. Let rest for 30 minutes in refrigerator. Prepare crepes as in basic crepe recipe.

CHOCOLATE CREAM CREPES:

Melt ¼ cup semi-sweet chocolate chip bits and let cool. Whip ¼ pint of heavy cream and stir in chocolate and 1 tablespoon Grand Marnier. Spread over dessert crepes and roll. Top with extra Chocolate Cream Sauce and strawberries.

CLAY POT

Cooking in clay pots has been done for centuries. There are a variety of these primitive looking pots on the market today. They have first been molded, then fired at a high temperature. Properly cared for, clay pots will last for years. Some pots are glazed, but the unglazed ones are better because the unfinished surface allows the pot to breathe.

Before using the pot, you must soak it in water for 10 minutes. This is often called "watering the pot." It allows the clay to absorb moisture, which seals the pot while cooking and prevents food from sticking.

Meat and vegetables are delicious when cooked in the clay pot. Nutrients and flavors are cooked in, and no oil or water is necessary, though either can be used if desired.

The clay-pot style of cooking is excellent for dieters since no fats are necessary. Clay pots are usually placed in unheated ovens and generally cook at a high temperature. This makes browning possible. If extra browning is needed, the top of the pot can be removed 5 minutes early. Turn on broiler for extra crispness.

To clean the pot just soak it in the sink and scrub with a strong brush. Rinse the pot with water and dry. Store the pot with the cover inverted on top of the pot.

Clay pots come in various sizes: for cooking for two, a medium-size pot will do, but for serving several people or to roast a turkey, you will need a large pot.

SWORDFISH STEAKS IN CLAY POT

4 6-ounce swordfish steaks
seasoned salt
½ pound sliced mushrooms
1 medium onion, sliced
1 teaspoon finely chopped parsley
2 tablespoons butter
1 cup dry white wine

Water pot for 10 minutes. Sprinkle fish with seasoned salt and place in pot. Top with mushrooms and onion. Sprinkle with parsley and dot with butter. Pour in wine. Cover. Place in preheated 425 F. oven and bake for 35 minutes.

Serves 4.

PORK CHOPS
WITH CABBAGE AND SOUR CREAM

1 small cabbage, cut into wedges
4 1-inch-thick pork chops
4 slices lemon
1 medium onion, chopped
2 cloves garlic, crushed
¼ teaspoon caraway seeds
¼ cup wine
⅔ cup sour cream
salt and pepper

Place cabbage in clay pot which has been watered for 10 minutes. Top with pork chops and place a slice of lemon on each chop. Sprinkle onion, garlic and caraway seeds over all, and pour in wine. Cover and place in unheated oven. Bake at 375 F. for 50 minutes. Transfer chops and cabbage to serving dish. Add sour cream to liquid and ingredients left in pot. Stir and season well with salt and pepper. Pour over pork and cabbage.

Serves 4.

CLAY POT CHICKEN WITH VEGETABLES

3 ¼ pound roasting chicken
1 teaspoon margarine
salt and pepper
4 carrots, scraped and quartered
4 stalks celery, trimmed and quartered
8 small white onions, peeled and left whole
¼ cup dry white wine
¼ teaspoon dried thyme

Water pot for 10 minutes. Rub chicken with margarine. Season chicken with salt and pepper. Place in pot. Surround chicken with vegetables and pour in white wine. Sprinkle with thyme. Cover and place in cold oven. Bake at 475 F. for 1 hour and 20 minutes. Remove vegetables to serving platter, return chicken to pot and place in oven, uncovered, and turn on broiler. Leave under broiler for about 5 minutes or until lightly browned.

Serves 4.

CLAY POT ROAST LEG OF LAMB

2 ½- to 3-pound leg of lamb
salt and freshly ground pepper
large clove of garlic, cut in half
½ teaspoon dry rosemary
8 small white onions, peeled
6 carrots, scraped and quartered

Water the pot. Rub salt, pepper, garlic and rosemary over lamb. Place in pot fat side up. Add onions and carrots. Cover and place in unheated oven and cook at 425 F. for 2 hours.

   Serves 6.

If you have another clay pot, you might want to serve baked potatoes with your lamb roast. Wash 6 potatoes and place them in the pot, which has been watered for 10 minutes. Cover pot and put in unheated oven. Bake at 450 F. for 35 minutes.

SLOW CROCK COOKER

Cooking in a crock pot is as old as clay pot cooking, but now electricity has been added. You can fill the pot, set it, and leave it unattended for several hours. You're free to go to work or do errands or just relax. When you return there is a hot, tasty meal waiting for you. There can't be an easier method of cooking.

The crock pot is a good friend to the inexperienced cook and is so convenient for singles, college students, vacationers, brides, working families and boaters.

Nutrients are preserved by cooking at low temperatures (200 F. to 300 F.), and meats cooked in the crock pot come out amazingly tender. Slow cooking in the crock pot is inexpensive because it uses about the same electricity as a 75 to 100 watt light bulb.

Because of its increasing popularity, there are many models available in various shapes and sizes. All come with their particular instructions for successful cooking. Regardless of your model, only a few basic rules need to be learned, aside from temperature information. After reading directions in your crock pot booklet remember the following: Do not turn on crock pot until food is in it. Don't lift lid until cooking is completed unless you must add ingredients. It takes 15 to 20 minutes to regain cooking temperature after the lid has been lifted. When food has cooked, turn dial to off and remove plug. Clean unit only after it has cooled.

Special recipes are required and here are some I collected for my book *The Slow Crock Cookbook.**

DAL

This is an unusual East Indian yellow-split-pea soup that will quickly become a favorite with family and guests.

> 1 pound dried yellow split peas
> 2 stalks celery, finely chopped
> 1 large carrot, finely chopped
> 1 medium onion, finely chopped
> 2 tablespoons butter
> 1 tablespoon curry powder
> 1 tablespoon lemon juice
> 1 bay leaf
> ½ teaspoon salt
> 3 chicken bouillon cubes
> 2 quarts water

Place all ingredients in crock pot and stir, cover, and cook on low for 7 to 9 hours. Garnish with chopped green pepper.

> *Serves 6 to 8.*
> *Cooking time: 7 to 9 hours.*

FLAGEOLETS À LA CROCK POT

These savory French beans are the classic accompaniment to roast leg of lamb. They are delicious when cooked in a slow crock cooker.

> 1 pound dried flageolets
> 2 cups chicken broth
> 3 cups water
> 1 onion, chopped
> 1 bay leaf
> ¼ teaspoon dried thyme
> pinch dried rosemary
> 1 teaspoon salt

Place ingredients in crock pot, cover, and cook on low for 8 to 10 hours.

> *Serves 8.*
> *Cooking time: 8 to 10 hours.*

COQ AU VIN

8 serving pieces chicken
salt and pepper
2 tablespoons butter
1 tablespoon oil
6 slices bacon, chopped
16 small white onions, peeled
2 cloves garlic, crushed
1 cup red Burgundy wine
1 cup beef stock
1 bay leaf
¼ teaspoon dried thyme
2 tablespoons tomato paste
1 8-ounce can whole tomatoes, chopped
salt and pepper to taste
¼ pound fresh mushrooms, sliced
fresh chopped parsley

Season chicken with salt and pepper. Heat butter and oil in large skillet, and brown chicken on both sides. Place in crock pot. Poach bacon in a cup of water in saucepan for 5 minutes. Drain and add to crock pot with remaining ingredients, except mushrooms and parsley. Cover and cook on low for 4 to 6 hours. Add mushrooms during last 20 minutes of cooking time. Garnish with parsley.

Serves 4.
Cooking time: 4 to 6 hours.

CHICKEN BREAST DINNER WITH LIMA BEANS

Crock pots are terrific for the single person, too.

1 whole chicken breast, halved
salt and pepper
1 tablespoon butter
1 tablespoon oil
1 large potato, cubed
½ package frozen lima beans, thawed
¼ cup chicken broth
⅛ teaspoon thyme
salt and pepper to taste

Season chicken with salt and pepper. Heat butter and oil in skillet, and brown chicken on both sides. Add to crock pot with remaining ingredients. Cover and cook on low for 4 to 6 hours. Serve with iced tea.

Serves 1.
Cooking time: 4 to 6 hours.

TURKEY LEGS WITH VEGETABLES

4 turkey legs
2 carrots, peeled and sliced into 1-inch lengths
2 potatoes, peeled and cubed
3 stalks celery, sliced
1 package dried onion soup mix
1 cup chicken stock
3 tablespoons dry white wine
1 bay leaf
½ teaspoon freshly ground pepper

Combine ingredients in crock pot, cover, and cook on low for 6 to 8 hours. Serve with rice or noodles.

Serves 4.
Cooking time: 6 to 8 hours.

SWISS STEAK

2 pounds round steak, cut into serving pieces
salt and pepper
3 tablespoons flour
2 tablespoons vegetable oil
1 16-ounce can tomatoes, chopped
1 medium-large onion
2 stalks celery, finely chopped
1 tablespoon prepared mustard
2 tablespoons wine vinegar
1 beef bouillon cube
1 tablespoon Worcestershire sauce
1 bay leaf
½ teaspoon salt

Season pieces of steak with salt and pepper. Dredge meat with flour. Heat oil in large skillet, and brown meat on each side. Add to crock pot with remaining ingredients. Cover and cook on low for 6 to 8 hours. Garnish with fresh chopped parsley. Serve with boiled potatoes.

Serves 4 to 6.
Cooking time: 6 to 8 hours.

WOK

The Chinese have been cooking in the wok for centuries, but Americans have only recently discovered its pleasures. As people learned more about Chinese cooking, they naturally wanted to duplicate their favorite Chinese dishes at home, and having a wok made that easy. The wok's curved shape resembles a bowl with handles. It can be made of iron, steel, stainless steel or aluminum. Iron is best. Woks come in a variety of sizes. The 14-inch wok is perfect for home use. Woks are sold in special food shops, department stores and in stores in Chinatown. Today they're often sold in sets that include the wok, cover, spoon and scoop with long handles and a metal ring to fit over home range electric or gas burners. The ring holds the wok in place, but it keeps the wok too far away from the heat to cook quickly enough for stir-frying. I don't use the ring except for deep-frying, steaming or making soup.

When stir-frying, which is the most common method of Chinese cooking, you must always hold the handle with a pot holder and stir with the scoop in the other hand if you don't use the metal ring. This may prove difficult at first, and for this reason I recommend buying a wok that comes with a long wood handle on one side. Also available are properly sized bamboo steamers which come in stacked sets with a lid. With the steamer you can steam dumplings or fish over water held in the wok. It's advised to use only 2 or 3 stacks when cooking at home. There are, of course, electric woks, but I don't recommend them because it is difficult to increase or decrease heat quickly enough for stir-frying, which is what you'll use your wok for most often.

The round shape of the wok distributes the heat evenly and this is essential in stir-frying. In this method, food that has been cut into small pieces is fried quickly in a little oil while being stirred constantly. Never cook large amounts of food in the wok. It will handle a dish for four only, containing no more than ¾ to 1 pound of sliced, diced or chopped meat plus other ingredients. If you're cooking for more than four, make the dish twice. Stir-frying takes only minutes.

The wok must be seasoned before it can be used. To do this wash the wok and dry it thoroughly. Put wok over heat and add 2 tablespoons vegetable or peanut oil. With wadded paper towels coat entire surface of wok with oil. Dry and repeat. When paper towels are clean after this process, it means all impurities have been removed. To clean wok after use simply fill with hot water and scour with stiff brush. Soap isn't necessary, but it can be used as long as wok is completely dried after use; otherwise it will rust. Your wok will begin to turn black in color as you use it. When this happens, as it should, it means you've become an old hand at wok cooking.

If you don't have a wok, a skillet is a fair substitute. And instead of the special spoon and scoop, a large spoon and spatula will do nicely.

CHEF MA'S SWEET AND SOUR PORK

I had the good fortune to spend a year working with Chef Ah-Yee Ma in his restaurant in Chinatown while writing a Chinese cookbook. Chef Ma was born in Nigpo and became a Master Chef at the age of twenty-two. He arrived in America in 1954 and headed the kitchens of several well-known restaurants in Washington, D.C., and New York before opening his own establishment, Chef Ma's, to great and well-earned success. The gentle and skilled Chef Ma patiently taught me the subtleties of Chinese cuisine. I was pleasantly surprised to learn the relative simplicity of the techniques of one of the finest schools of cooking in the world. Sweet and Sour Pork is an American favorite of Chinese food lovers. Two cooking procedures are used in this dish, but it takes only minutes to produce this delicious Chinese standard.

1-pound pork tenderloin, cut into 1-inch cubes
2 tablespoons sherry
2 tablespoons soy sauce
¼ teaspoon powdered ginger (use ½ teaspoon grated
    fresh ginger if available)
½ cup cornstarch
2 cups peanut oil
2 carrots, peeled and cut into 1½-inch sticks
1 large green pepper, seeded and cut into 1-inch squares
1 medium-large onion, cut into large slivers
1 large clove garlic, minced
3 tablespoons ketchup
2 tablespoons soy sauce
2 tablespoons sugar
2 tablespoons vinegar
salt
1 cup chicken stock
1½ tablespoons cornstarch dissolved in 2 tablespoons
    water
1 8-ounce can pineapple chunks, drained

Combine sherry, soy sauce and ginger in medium-size bowl.
Add pork cubes, toss until each piece of pork is coated with mixture. Sprinkle with 1 tablespoon cornstarch, toss again. Cover and
refrigerate for 30 minutes. Dust each piece of pork with cornstarch
and fry, a few pieces at a time in hot peanut oil in a wok or skillet.
Drain and pour off all of oil except for 2 tablespoons. Add carrots,
green pepper, onion and garlic. Stir-fry or toss in wok for 3 minutes. Add remaining ingredients except for cornstarch, pineapple
and pork. Stir until sauce is well combined. Add water and cornstarch mixture and stir until sauce thickens. Finally, add pineapple chunks and pork and gently toss until well heated.

Serve over hot fluffy rice.
Serves 4.

CHICKEN AND CASHEWS

1½ cups diced raw chicken
½ egg white
1 teaspoon soy sauce
1 teaspoon cornstarch
1 cup oil
1 cup broth, heated
½ teaspoon sesame oil
½ teaspoon sugar
¼ teaspoon MSG (optional)
1 tablespoon cornstarch mixed with 2 tablespoons water
⅔ cup natural cashews

PREPARATION:
Mix chicken with egg white, soy sauce and cornstarch. Place in small bowl, cover and refrigerate for ½ hour. Have remaining ingredients measured and ready to use.

TO COOK:
Heat oil in wok and add chicken. Stir-fry until meat is no longer pink. Remove with strainer and drain. Transfer oil except for 2 tablespoons to container and save for later use. Return chicken to wok and add broth, sesame oil, sugar, MSG (if used) and toss for 15 seconds. Now add cornstarch mixture and stir. Add nuts. Toss for about 20 seconds until nuts are heated through.

Serves 4.

STIR-FRIED SHRIMP AND PEAS

2 tablespoons peanut oil
¾ pound medium shrimp, shelled and deveined
1 clove garlic, crushed
1 tablespoon soy sauce
½ cup chicken broth
1 cup green peas
2 teaspoons cornstarch mixed with 2 teaspoons water

Heat oil in wok or skillet and add shrimp. Stir-fry for 2 minutes. Remove shrimp and add garlic and stir for 20 seconds. Add shrimp, soy sauce, chicken broth and toss for 1 minute. Stir in green peas and cornstarch mixture and stir-fry until sauce thickens.

Serves 4.

SHREDDED BEEF WITH BLACK BEAN SAUCE

½ pound shredded flank steak
1 tablespoon cornstarch
3 tablespoons peanut oil
*2 tablespoons black bean sauce ***
1 cup sliced mushrooms
⅓ cup sliced water chestnuts
1 tablespoon soy sauce
½ cup chicken broth
2 teaspoons cornstarch mixed with 2 teaspoons water

Mix cornstarch and beef and refrigerate for ½ hour. Heat oil in wok or skillet and add beef. Stir-fry for 3 minutes. Add black bean sauce, mushrooms, water chestnuts and soy sauce. Stir-fry for 1 minute. Add chicken broth and stir. Finally add cornstarch mixture and stir until sauce thickens.

Serves 4.

MICROWAVE OVEN

One of the most innovative cooking appliances of our time is the microwave oven. I think of microwave cooking as space-age cooking and that it is about as appealing to the creative cook as those other wonders of space-ship living—powdered orange juice and food in tubes.

Microwaves are short electromagnetic waves. A microwave oven is a metal oven that contains a magnetron tube which produces magnetic waves that penetrate and cook the food quickly. There are over 20 different models and each manufacturer offers special

---

*Available in Chinese or specialty food market.

cooking instructions for their model. The food being cooked reacts to the heat according to its weight and shape. With a leg of lamb, for instance, it is difficult to assure even cooking, because one end is thicker than the other. But most food does cook quickly, and I can understand why this process appeals to busy people. You can't learn to cook with a microwave oven, but you can produce a fast product. Even if you are fascinated by such gadgetry, it is expensive. If you are willing to spend that kind of money on a culinary item, your money will be better spent buying a food processor.

To be fair, there are advantages to microwave cooking. Food can be thawed and cooked in minutes. A turkey roasts in half an hour. The microwave oven is fine for heating food such as soup and sandwiches in only 1 minute. The kitchen stays cool while the food cooks in the oven, and the food can be cooked in serving dishes—thus saving on pots and pans and dishwashing. The cooking foods will heat the dishes they are in only a small amount. Metal pans reflect the microwaves and can't be used in these ovens. Glass, china, plastic and paper are all safe.

The disadvantages of this kind of cooking far outweigh the advantages, I believe. Food will not brown or broil no matter what certain manufacturers claim. There is little room for creativity, and testing and tasting and slow basting is out. Despite safety devices, the oven should be off limits for children unless an adult is in the kitchen with them to check that latches and dials are set correctly.

As for safety standards, they are set by the government and the F.C.C. controls microwave frequencies by law. It is essential that the door on a microwave oven fit properly so that the energy is confined to the inside of the oven. Some manufacturers have had to recall ovens because of faulty doors. So choose carefully.

chapter 2. hors d'oeuvres
first courses
soups

HORS D'OEUVRES

The hors d'oeuvres, or appetizers, set the stage and mood for the rest of a meal, so it's vital that they are well made and attractive. Serve piping hot if a hot dish or well chilled if a cold dish. Since they are the beginning, you don't want them to be "too much"— in taste or quantity—or the rest of the meal will be anti-climactic. Make them interesting and enticing, but not overpowering.

You can produce a great cocktail party with four or five of these appetizers; for example, shrimp toast, rumaki, hummus, raw fresh vegetables and caviar dip and cereal scramble go well together. Serve the various appetizers in appealing bowls and platters of proper size. Appetizers should never be crushed together. Garnish the dishes with little bouquets of fresh parsley, watercress, and lemon wedges sprinkled with paprika.

Most men would agree that the opening move is often significant in games or business, and so it is with food.

GEORGE NELSON'S TARTAR STEAK

George Nelson, president of the George Nelson Fund, is a dedicated gourmet. He belongs to ten gastronomical societies, and is co-founder of the Ambassadeurs du Bien Manger, a small circle of business, professional and diplomatic gourmets who gather periodically to partake of a dinner prepared by professional chefs.

Since he appreciates fine food faultlessly prepared he rarely cooks himself because, as he put it, "As much as I love music, I abandoned the piano years ago because I could not stand the sound I made."

> 2 pounds top round or filet mignon (meat should be
> ground only ½ hour before preparing or see in-
> structions below*)

*If the meat was not ground ½ hour before serving, it will need to be rescued by the addition of:

> 1 tablespoon vinegar
> 1½ teaspoons Worcestershire sauce
> 3 tablespoons oil
> 1 teaspoon vodka

Combine thoroughly before adding to steak recipe.

4 egg yolks
1 medium onion, finely chopped
salt and pepper to taste
¼ teaspoon paprika
4 teaspoons crushed capers
½ tablespoon mild mustard
fresh chopped parsley

Place ground meat in large bowl and add egg yolks, onion, salt, pepper, paprika, capers, mustard and mix well. Shape into large patties and garnish with parsley. Serve on toast or sour rye bread.

Serves 4.

RAW FRESH VEGETABLES AND RED CAVIAR DIP

Appetizers can be a problem if you have decided to entertain at the last minute and don't want to be in the kitchen preparing a dish when your guests arrive. Raw fresh vegetables are a welcome appetizer, too often neglected, and take almost no preparation time.

1 pound thin asparagus stalks, washed and ends cut off
1 pint cherry tomatoes
2 cups large black olives
1 small head cauliflower, broken into small flowerets

RED CAVIAR DIP:

½ pint sour cream
2-ounce jar red caviar
1 scallion, minced
1 teaspoon lemon juice

Combine ingredients and serve in small bowl with vegetables arranged attractively around it on platter.

Serves 8 to 10 as appetizer.

RUMAKI

½ pound bacon
1 7-ounce can water chestnuts, cut into ¼-inch slices
¾ pound chicken livers, cut into bite-size pieces
½ cup soy sauce
2 tablespoons oil
2 scallions, chopped
1 clove garlic, crushed
½ teaspoon sugar
2 tablespoons sherry

Cut bacon in half. Wrap slice of bacon around 1 slice of water chestnut and piece of chicken liver. Secure with toothpick. Repeat procedure until all bacon is used. Mix remaining ingredients in bowl and add Rumaki. Toss until all pieces are coated with mixture. Cover and refrigerate for 1 hour. Drain and place on baking sheet covered with foil. Broil until bacon is cooked on all sides.

This is also delicious without the chicken livers.

Serves 8 to 10.

PAUL GITLIN'S CHOPPED CHICKEN LIVER

When Paul Gitlin, the author's attorney, was first married, his initial foray into the kitchen produced this chopped chicken liver recipe.

1 tablespoon rendered chicken fat
3 tablespoons vegetable oil
1 pound chicken livers (cleaned and trimmed)
1 medium-large onion, chopped
3 hard-boiled eggs
salt
freshly ground pepper

Heat rendered chicken fat and oil in skillet. Cook chicken livers in mixture, stirring constantly, for about 4 minutes. Add onion and cook 5 minutes. Put liver and onion through meat grinder or chop up in wooden bowl with double-bladed chopper. Place in another bowl. Grind or finely chop hard-boiled eggs. Combine eggs with liver mixture and season with salt and pepper.

Zelda, Paul's wife, added the garnishes:
Place mound of chopped liver on serving dish. Garnish with sprigs of parsley, celery sticks, radishes and green pepper strips. Accompany with black bread, Thin Crisps or other crackers.

Serves 4 to 6.

DEVILED EGGS WITH CURRY

8 hard-boiled eggs
1 teaspoon prepared mustard
2 teaspoons vinegar
¼ cup mayonnaise
1 teaspoon freshly chopped parsley
1 teaspoon curry powder
1 tablespoon grated onion
1 tablespoon grated green pepper

Cut eggs in half lengthwise. Carefully remove yolks and place in bowl. Add remaining ingredients to yolks and mix well. Spoon mixture into egg whites and sprinkle with paprika.

Serves 4 to 6.

MARINATED MUSHROOMS

1 pound mushrooms
½ cup vegetable oil
2 tablespoons lemon juice
½ teaspoon dried oregano
½ teaspoon fresh chopped parsley
1 scallion, minced
2 tablespoons minced pimento
½ teaspoon salt
½ teaspoon ground pepper

Combine ingredients in glass or ceramic bowl. Cover and refrigerate for several hours.

Serves 4 to 6.

MUSHROOM STUFFED MUSHROOMS

24 large fresh mushroom caps
1 pound mushrooms, wiped clean, stem ends cut off
3 shallots
4 tablespoons butter
2 tablespoons flour
1 cup milk, scalded
½ teaspoon dried tarragon
1 teaspoon freshly chopped parsley
½ teaspoon salt
freshly ground pepper to taste
¼ cup Cheddar cheese, shredded
bread crumbs

Finely chop the pound of mushrooms and shallots. Or, using steel knife of the Cuisinart food processor, process mushrooms and shallots. Place mixture in clean dish towel and wring until most of moisture is removed from mushrooms. Add 2 tablespoons of butter to skillet and saute mushroom mixture until the mushrooms have dried slightly and begin to separate. Remove from heat. In clean saucepan heat 2 tablespoons butter and add flour, stirring constantly. Slowly pour in scalded milk, always stirring with whisk. Add half of sauce to mushroom mixture with tarragon, chopped parsley, salt, pepper and cheese. Stir until cheese is melted. Add as much remaining sauce as possible, but maintain a thick-stuffing-like consistency. Stuff mushroom caps with mixture and sprinkle bread crumbs on top. Place on well-buttered baking sheet and bake in 350 F. oven for 15 minutes until tops brown nicely.

Serves 8.

LOWELL WEICKER'S MOCK CHEESE BLINTZES

Senator Lowell Weicker of Connecticut says, "Cooking is one of my favorite hobbies—it's just great fun to get in the kitchen, make a mess and hope that something new and different will result. Since I'm not able to spend as much time as I'd like experimenting in the kitchen, I often depend on my tried and true quickies. This is one of those that is really a snap to make. In fact, I've served it at my staff parties and when my press secretary, who is nothing short of a gourmet, complimented this dessert, I knew I'd finally made it on the culinary scene!"

> 2 loaves of unsliced white bread
> 1 pound of cream cheese, at room temperature
> 2 egg yolks
> ¼ cup sugar
> 1 pound butter
> sugar
> cinnamon

Slice bread into 7 strips lengthwise. Cut off crust and roll out each slice with a rolling pin to flatten bread. In a bowl beat together the cream cheese, egg yolks and sugar. Spread mixture onto each slice of bread and then roll up each slice as you would a jelly roll. Set aside. Next, melt butter and add sugar and cinnamon to taste. Brush this mixture on each jelly roll, including the ends of the rolls. Cool and freeze rolls. Remove rolls from the freezer as needed and slice into ½-inch slices 5 to 10 minutes before serving. Place on foil-covered cookie sheets and place in hot oven for 5 to 10 minutes. Serve with sour cream.

> *Serves 12 to 14.*

HUMMUS

If you like chick peas, you'll love hummus. It's a quick and unusual appetizer.

> 1-pound can chick peas, drained
> 2 cloves garlic, crushed
> ½ cup Taheeni* (sesame seed paste)
> 2 tablespoons lemon juice
> salt
> olive oil

Place chick peas in bowl and crush with fork. Add garlic, Taheeni, lemon juice, and salt to taste. Mix well. Moisten with several

---

* Available in specialty food shops.

drops of olive oil until still firm but smooth. Adjust seasoning to your taste.

Serve with pita (Middle Eastern flat bread) or raw vegetables.

Serves 6 to 8 as appetizer.

GUACAMOLE

2 ripe avocados, peeled and seeds removed
2 scallions, finely chopped
1 large tomato, peeled and chopped
2 cloves garlic, crushed
½ teaspoon salt
½ teaspoon chili powder
dash Tabasco sauce
1 tablespoon lemon juice or to taste
freshly ground pepper

Place avocado in bowl and mash the pulp with the back of a fork. Add remaining ingredients and stir vigorously. Cover and refrigerate for 1 hour before serving. Check seasoning.

Serve with taco chips or fresh vegetables.

Serves 6 to 8 as appetizer.

ROBERT GINSBERG'S AVOCADO LOG

Gourmets Bobby and Sheila Ginsberg have traveled all over the world to be able to taste the finest foods. They are indefatigable in their search. For instance, after they finally located a highly recommended restaurant in Taipeh, they willingly endured several hours of waiting, without appetizer or libation, in a stuffy curtained compartment, to be able to taste a single specialty. Their patience was rewarded with the most succulent Peking Duck they have ever experienced.

At home, Sheila's the cook and Bobby's the gardener. Bobby did once experience a spiritual moment in the kitchen, however. He bought two ripe avocados so that he could plant the seeds, but he didn't know what

to do with the velvet pulp. He emptied it into a bowl and did some
improvising. The following recipe is the easy and delicious result.

> 2 ripe avocados
> 8 ounces cream cheese, at room temperature
> ½ cup grated Cheddar cheese
> 1 cup finely chopped cashews
> 4 teaspoons lime juice
> 3 tablespoons chopped parsley
> 1 teaspoon Worcestershire Sauce
> dash of Tabasco Sauce
> salt, pepper and garlic powder to taste
> paprika

Combine avocados, cream cheese, Cheddar cheese, chopped
cashews and lime juice in large bowl. Add remaining ingredients
into mix and shape with hands into a long, narrow roll. Place on
dish, cover and refrigerate for at least 3 hours. Decorate by rolling
in paprika. Roll can also be garnished with olive slices, fresh dill
weed or thin cucumber slices across top of roll.

> *Serves 8 to 10 as appetizer.*

SHRIMP TOAST

> 1 pound raw shrimp, shelled and deveined
> 4 scallions, minced
> ½ cup minced water chestnuts
> 1 egg, lightly beaten
> 1½ tablespoons soy sauce
> 1 tablespoon cornstarch
> 1 teaspoon salt
> pinch of ginger
> 12 slices day-old white bread, crusts trimmed off
> plain dry bread crumbs
> vegetable oil

Place shrimp in Cuisinart food processor or blender (puree a few
at a time) and process for about 20 seconds. Remove shrimp to

bowl and add scallions, water chestnuts, egg, soy sauce, cornstarch, salt and ginger. Mix well and spread in equal amounts on bread. Sprinkle with bread crumbs. Heat about ¾ inch oil in large skillet and fry shrimp toast, shrimp side down, a few slices at a time until golden. Turn and cook until golden. Drain. Cut each piece of toast in half diagonally, twice.

Serve with lemon wedges.

Serves 8.

ED COHEN'S CHEESE PUFFS

Ed Cohen, a hairdresser, claims: "Cooking is a good excuse for taking out your frustrations from daily routines. It also helps to make good conversation. My kitchen is the center of my parties. That is, people always seem to gravitate to a nice warm, friendly kitchen. Everyone enjoys food and likes talking about it."

> 1 cup water
> ½ cup (1 stick) margarine
> 1 cup flour (Ed uses Wondra flour)
> 1 teaspoon salt
> 1 teaspoon dry mustard
> 4 eggs
> ¼ teaspoon cayenne pepper (optional)
> 1 cup shredded Cheddar cheese, about 4 ounces

Heat water and margarine in a large saucepan and bring to a full boil. Add flour, which has been mixed with salt and mustard, all at once. Stir vigorously with a wooden spoon until mixture forms a thick, smooth ball and leaves the sides of the pan clean. Remove from heat; cool slightly. Add eggs, one at a time, beating well after each addition until paste is shiny and smooth. Stir in cayenne and cheese. Fill a pastry tube fitted with a notched tip. Press out into small puffs about 1 rounded teaspoon for each puff, 1½ inches apart on a lightly greased cookie sheet. Bake in preheated 400 F. oven about 25 minutes or until puffs are golden and swollen. Remove puffs to wire rack and serve while still hot.

Makes about 24 puffs.

SAUTEED ALMONDS

2 tablespoons clarified butter (see index for recipe)
10 ounces blanched almonds
salt to taste

Heat butter in skillet and add almonds. Over medium-low heat, saute almonds, stirring frequently, until lightly browned on both sides. Transfer to plate lined with paper towels. Sprinkle lightly with salt. With another piece of paper towel blot off butter and put in nut dish. Serve while still warm.

Serves 6 as appetizer.

CEREAL SCRAMBLE

1 pound mixed salted nuts
3 cups Cheerios cereal
2 cups Wheat Chex cereal
2 cups stick pretzels
3 tablespoons vegetable oil
3 tablespoons Worcestershire sauce
salt if needed

Mix together ingredients in large shallow baking pan. Bake in preheated 275 F. oven for 45 minutes, stirring mixture with wooden spoon every 15 minutes.

Makes about 2½ quarts.

FIRST COURSES

MUSSELS

Mussels are great as an appetizer, first course, or main dish. I can't urge you enough to investigate these inexpensive, easy-to-prepare mollusks.

I once talked about the virtues of mussels on a television show and later received a threatening letter from a friend. He warned me to stop telling people how wonderful mussels are or their price would go up.

I prefer fresh live mussels, but they are available plain and smoked in jars and cans. Cleaning mussels takes a little time, but the procedure is simple. Call to the family or guests for help.

Wash the mussels in cool running water. Clean them with a stiff brush and remove the beard (byssus) by pulling it off with your thumb and forefinger. Throw away any mussels that don't open after they are cooked. For first course:

> 3 to 4 pounds mussels, cleaned
> 1 cup dry white wine
> 1 cup water

In a large pot, steam mussels for 5 or 6 minutes in white wine and water. Serve hot with garlic butter, lemon wedges and sprigs of parsley.

> Serves 10 to 12.

MARINATED MUSSELS

> 3 to 4 pounds mussels, scrubbed and debearded
> 1/2 cup dry white wine
> 2/3 cup olive oil
> 3 tablespoons lemon juice
> 1/4 cup fresh chopped parsley
> 1 large clove garlic, crushed
> 1/2 teaspoon salt
> 1/2 teaspoon dry mustard
> freshly ground pepper to taste

Place cleaned mussels in large pot with wine and 1 cup water. Bring to a boil and cook for about 6 minutes, until mussel shells open. Discard empty halves of mussel shells and any unopened mussels. Arrange shells on large platter. Place remaining ingredients in blender and puree for 20 seconds. Spoon over mussels and let sit for 3 hours at room temperature.

> Serves 10 to 12.

BAKED CLAMS

16 hard-shell clams, well scrubbed
2 tablespoons olive oil
1 tablespoon butter
2 tablespoons finely chopped shallots or onion
2 cloves garlic, minced
2 tablespoons finely chopped parsley
½ teaspoon dried basil
½ teaspoon dried oregano
½ cup dry bread crumbs
2 tablespoons freshly grated Parmesan cheese
2 tablespoons dry white wine
salt and freshly ground pepper to taste

Place clams in pot and add ¾ cup water, cover and cook for about 6 to 8 minutes until clams open. Remove clams. When cool enough to handle, remove empty top shells. In skillet, heat oil and butter. Saute shallots or onion for 3 minutes. Add remaining ingredients and stir until well cooked. Mixture should be moist, but not soggy. If too dry, add a little clam juice. Top each clam with mixture and place on baking sheet. Bake in preheated 400 F. oven for 5 minutes, then place under broiler until golden.

Serves 4.

MAURICE EVANS' SALMON MOUSSE

Maurice Evans, the actor, who employs a full-time cook, lives in Surrey, England. When he was in New York recently, I asked him for his version of "The Ultimate Meal." Although he was expecting guests for dinner that night and leaving on a cruise the next morning, he also graciously gave me the recipe for his Salmon Mousse.

1 pound can salmon, drained, skin and bones removed
8-ounce can evaporated milk
1 envelope plain gelatin
2 tablespoons chopped parsley
1 tablespoon chopped dill
1 teaspoon dry mustard
salt and freshly ground pepper to taste
½ cucumber, peeled and thinly sliced

Place evaporated milk in blender, blend on high for 30 seconds. In 3 tablespoons of cold water dissolve gelatin in small pot over hot water. Add salmon, gelatin and all other ingredients to evaporated milk, except for cucumbers, and blend on low for 30 seconds. Wet a metal mold (preferably fish-shaped). Put mixture into mold and refrigerate overnight. Unmold and garnish with cucumbers as if fish scales. Use slice of stuffed olive for fish eye and surround with watercress.

Serves 6.

SHRIMP WITH COCKTAIL DIP

1 pound fresh boiled shrimp (See index for recipe)

DIP:
¾ cup mayonnaise
¼ cup ketchup
juice of 1 lemon
1 teaspoon horseradish
dash of Tabasco sauce

Combine ingredients, cover and refrigerate for several hours.

Yield: about 1 cup.

AVOCADO VINAIGRETTE

This simple dish deserves mention here because of its instant preparation. Keep Avocado Vinaigrette in mind, either as a first course or a salad, when you're planning a special, but quick dinner.

2 large ripe avocados
2 teaspoons lemon juice
¾ cup Vinaigrette Sauce (See index for recipe)

Cut avocados in half and remove seeds. Brush surface of pulp with lemon juice to keep avocado from discoloring. Spoon equal amounts of sauce in hole in avocado halves.

Serves 4.

HARRY RIGBY'S SHRIMP EVIN*

Harry Rigby is a theatrical producer who loves food. His family had a cook most of the time while he was growing up, but when the cook left, his mother claimed to be allergic to gas and he was forced to attempt cooking. The one cookbook in the house was far too complicated for a beginner. He finally found a cookbook with easy directions to follow and still cherishes its foxed pages. Now, Harry is so fond of cooking that he will gladly devote a whole day to the preparation of a good dinner—a dinner that might begin with Shrimp Evin.

> 2 pounds medium cooked shrimp, shelled and deveined
> ¼ cup red wine vinegar
> ¾ cup olive oil
> 10 shallots, finely chopped
> juice of 1 lemon
> 1 tablespoon chopped parsley
> freshly ground pepper
> 1 tablespoon freshly chopped dill weed (optional)

Combine ingredients, cover and refrigerate all day or overnight. Drain well and arrange on lettuce leaves on serving platter or individual plates. If desired, you can squeeze a little more fresh lemon juice over shrimp.

Serves 6.

SHRIMP CANAPES WITH HERB BUTTER

> 6-ounce jar tiny Danish shrimp, drained
> 1 stick butter, at room temperature
> 1 tablespoon fresh chopped parsley
> ½ teaspoon dried tarragon
> 1 tablespoon chopped chives
> 1 teaspoon lemon juice
> 24 slices pumpernickel party bread rounds

Mix butter, parsley, tarragon, chives and lemon juice. Spread on bread. Top with 2 shrimp per slice.

Serves 8 to 10.

* Evin, aged 2, is the son of Mary Jo and Charles Dobson. He is the model for the silhouette logo of Dobson's restaurant in Manhattan.

MARVIN PAIGE'S SHRIMP RÉMOULADE

Restaurant operation consultant Marvin Paige is also a wholesale seafood dealer. He guided me through the fascinating Fulton Fish Market at 5 A.M. one day while I was researching a seafood cookbook. Naturally, he's very fond of seafood. He thinks New York restaurants offer the best food in this country, but he admits you can get some great meals in New Orleans. Several years ago, after tasting the spicy Shrimp Rémoulade served in New Orleans' famous Arnaud's restaurant, Marvin began experimenting to duplicate the dish. Finally, he was happy when New Orleans friends agreed his was as good as Arnaud's.

1½ pounds medium shrimp, shelled and deveined
1 bay leaf
2 tablespoons lemon juice
¼ teaspoon salt
5 peppercorns
1 bunch scallions, chopped
2 stalks celery, chopped
1 tablespoon capers
2 tablespoons finely chopped parsley (use Italian parsley, if available.)
3 tablespoons Creole mustard*
1 teaspoon white horseradish
2 tablespoons paprika
½ teaspoon white pepper
1 teaspoon salt
pinch cayenne pepper
2 tablespoons lemon juice
⅓ cup white vinegar
½ teaspoon dried basil
1 cup peanut oil
4 large lettuce leaves

Place shrimp in saucepan with bay leaf, lemon juice, salt and peppercorns. Cover the shrimp with water and bring to a boil. Reduce heat to a low boil and cook for 5 minutes. Remove shrimp and drain. Place shrimp in bowl, cover and refrigerate for at least 2 hours. Take 1 teaspoon each of chopped scallions, celery, capers

---

* Marvin uses Reeves Creole Mustard, but if you can't find a Creole Mustard, use your favorite hot mustard.

and parsley and set aside. Place remaining scallions, celery, capers and parsley in a blender or food processor and puree. Transfer mixture to bowl and add mustard, horseradish, paprika, white pepper, salt, and cayenne pepper. Blend with spoon. Now add lemon juice, vinegar and basil. Slowly beat in oil. Add reserved chopped scallions, celery, capers, parsley and shrimp. Mix well, cover and refrigerate for 2 hours. Stir well, again, and serve on lettuce leaves.

Serves 4.

This dish is very spicy. To reduce the fire, omit some horse-radish and cayenne pepper.

SOUPS

Few dishes are as satisfying on a cold winter's day as a steaming bowl of hearty soup, or as refreshing on a hot sultry day as a well-flavored chilled soup. And there isn't a dish easier to prepare. Making soup is also an excellent way to exercise your own creativity in the kitchen. Concoct a soup all your own with seasonal vegetables or any favorite ingredient. The essential point to remember about soup making is to use cool water and add the other ingredients before heating the liquid. The cool water, as it heats, helps draw out the flavor of the ingredients into the liquid and insures a tasty soup. (The opposite method is used for cooking vegetables; add the vegetables to boiling water to lock the flavor into them.)

Bonne soupe!

CROUTONS

Croutons are crunchy little cubes of golden toasted or fried bread that serve as a garnish for most soups. They are also excellent additions to most salads.

Of course, you can buy the boxed variety, but they aren't nearly as good as the home-made kind. What food ever is?

TOASTED CROUTONS

Cut day-old white sandwich, French, or two-day-old home-made white bread into ½-inch cubes. Spread out on cookie sheet and place in preheated 350 F. oven. Bake until golden, stirring occasionally. Make only 2 cups at a time.

FRIED CROUTONS

⅔ cup vegetable or peanut oil
2 tablespoons butter (clarified, if possible)
1 to 2 cups ½-inch bread cubes

Heat oil and butter in medium skillet and fry cubes, stirring gently, until crisp and golden. Remove with slotted spoon and drain on absorbent paper.

To make herbed croutons: Mix ½ teaspoon each of chopped parsley, oregano and basil, ¼ teaspoon garlic powder and salt and pepper to taste in small bowl. Sprinkle mixture over toasted or fried croutons and toss.

KEVIN H. WHITE'S FISH CHOWDER

Kevin H. White is the mayor of Boston. To quote him: "Boston is a small town, really more a collection of neighborhoods than a city. A political candidate in Boston has the best of all possible worlds to demonstrate his gastronomic commitment to every conceivable bloc. He is allowed to enjoy the Italian cooking of the North End, the delicacies of Chinatown, the superb seafood of Boston's waterfront landmarks, the meats, fresh vegetables and flowers in Faneuil Market, the soul food of Roxbury and the stews of Southie. They all make up the grand buffet that is this great city.

"My favorite dish (it was John F. Kennedy's, too), is fish chowder. President Kennedy was so addicted to the fish chowder served at Jimmy's Harborside Restaurant that he had it shipped to him in Thermos bottles during his travels. What chili is to Texans and chicken soup is to New Yorkers, fish chowder is to Boston's Irish politicians."

2 pounds haddock bones and skins
1½ quarts water
3 tablespoons butter
1 medium onion, finely chopped
2 tablespoons flour
¾ pound thick haddock filets, cut into small pieces
1 pint light cream
salt and freshly ground pepper to taste

Place haddock bones and skins in cold water and bring to a boil. Reduce heat and simmer for about 45 minutes until reduced to 1 quart of fish stock. Strain and reserve broth. Heat butter and saute onion for 5 minutes. Sprinkle with flour and cook for 3 or 4 minutes, stirring. Slowly pour in hot fish stock, constantly stirring. Add pieces of haddock, cover and simmer until haddock flakes easily, about 10 minutes. Add light cream and season well with salt and pepper. Heat chowder until almost boiling, remove from heat and serve immediately.

Serves 4.

OYSTER STEW

2 dozen oysters, removed from shells, and their liquid
3 tablespoons butter
2 cups milk
2½ cups light cream
½ teaspoon salt
freshly ground pepper to taste
extra butter

Simmer oysters in their own juice with 3 tablespoons butter in saucepan until edges curl. Scald milk and cream and pour over oysters. Season well with salt and pepper. Place pat of butter on each serving and accompany with oyster crackers.

Serves 4.

MINESTRONE

2 tablespoons vegetable oil
1 medium-large onion, chopped
1 large clove garlic, minced
2 stalks celery, chopped
1½ quarts water
1 quart beef stock
2 cups canned chick peas
1½ cups shredded cabbage
1-pound can whole tomatoes, chopped
1 medium zucchini, sliced and halved
1 tablespoon fresh chopped parsley
1 teaspoon dried basil
½ teaspoon dried oregano
salt and pepper to taste
1 cup macaroni
grated Parmesan cheese (fresh, if possible)

Heat oil in heavy pot. Saute onion and garlic for 5 minutes. Add remaining ingredients except for macaroni and Parmesan cheese. Bring to a boil and simmer for 30 minutes. Add macaroni and cook for 30 minutes. Serve with grated Parmesan cheese.

Serves 8.

BERNARD GREBANIER'S SOUPE AU PISTOU

Bernard Grebanier taught and directed most of Shakespeare's plays. He wrote over thirty books, his last being Then Came Each Actor. *He also wrote poetry, played the piano and cooked with considerable authority.*

I was fortunate enough to study Shakespeare under Professor Grebanier and, as an added bonus, acquired two of his prized recipes for this cookbook.

"This is my variation of an old Provençal soup. Pistou is the Provençal word for pestle. It's a heavenly soup."

¼ cup dried white marrow beans
¼ cup dried fava beans (These can be bought in Italian
    food stores or substitute large lima beans.)
¼ cup dried kidney beans
¼ cup dried cecci (garbanzos)
2½ quarts chicken stock
1 tablespoon salt
¼ teaspoon freshly grated pepper
12 cloves of garlic
3 teaspoons fresh basil
3 tablespoons vegetable or olive oil
stale bread

Place beans in water in large pot and allow to soak overnight. The next day drain beans, add stock and bring to a boil. Simmer slowly for 2½ hours, having added salt and pepper. Take off 2 cups of stock and set aside. Crush garlic cloves in mortar with pestle or use blender. Add basil and oil and continue mashing or blending. Bring the reserved 2 cups of soup stock to a boil in a small pan and add garlic mixture. Stir and place in serving bowl. At the bottom of each soup plate put a piece of stale bread, then ladle on the bean soup, and top with a few spoonfuls of pistou (i.e. the garlic, basil, oil and soup mixture).

Serves 6.

QUICK GREEN PEA SOUP

1 quart chicken broth
2 10-ounce packages frozen green peas
1 medium onion, chopped
½ teaspoon dried oregano
freshly ground pepper

Bring chicken broth to a boil. Add green peas, onion, oregano and pepper. Simmer for 5 minutes. Puree soup in blender, 2 cupfuls at a time. Check seasoning.

Serves 4 to 6.

SPLIT PEA SOUP

2 cups dried split peas
1 ham bone
1 large onion, chopped
2 carrots, peeled and chopped
¼ teaspoon dried thyme
1 teaspoon salt
freshly ground pepper to taste
1½ quarts water
1 quart chicken stock

Place ingredients in large heavy pot. Bring to a boil, reduce heat and simmer for 1½ to 2 hours. Discard ham bone.
Garnish with fried sliced sausage.

Serves 8.

QUICK BLACK BEAN SOUP

1 10-ounce can black bean soup
1 can water
1 tablespoon sherry
1 cup sour cream
4 lemon slices

In saucepan heat black bean soup and water. Stir until smooth and hot. Add sherry and remove from heat. Stir in ¾ cup sour cream. Ladle into soup bowls and garnish with a dollop of sour cream and lemon slice.

Serves 4.

RICHARD LEVI'S THICK LENTIL SOUP

My brother-in-law, Richard Levi, alas, doesn't have much time for cooking. He did make square hamburgers for dinner one night and son Steven said they were very weird. So he stopped cooking until his wife, Suzanne, was in the hospital giving birth to their son Jamie. The day she returned home, Richard decided to surprise her with a meal of lentil soup. It was a disaster. He made up a recipe using lentils, fatty beef bones, lots of water and little seasoning. The worse it tasted, the longer he cooked it, and where it ended up we will not divulge here. There's a happy ending to this story. Over the years since Jamie's birth, Dick's been working on his lentil soup recipe. I tested his latest and it's terrific.

> 1 pound dried lentils
> 2 quarts water
> 2 cups beef bouillon
> 1 large onion, chopped
> 2 stalks celery, chopped
> 3 carrots, peeled and diced
> 1 medium potato, peeled and cubed
> 1 pound lean spare ribs, cut into 2 rib pieces
> 1 bay leaf
> ½ teaspoon dried thyme
> 2 teaspoons salt or to taste
> freshly ground pepper to taste
> 1 1-pound can whole tomatoes

Place all ingredients except for tomatoes in large pot. Bring to a boil, reduce heat and simmer for 1 hour. Remove ribs and cool until they can be handled. Continue cooking soup over very low flame in the meantime. Cut meat off bones and chop into small pieces. With large spoon, remove any fat on surface of soup. Return meat to soup with chopped tomatoes and juice from can. Cook for 30 minutes longer. Remove two cups of soup from pot and puree in blender or food mill. Return pureed soup to pot and adjust seasoning, if necessary.

Serves 6 to 8.

CORN CHOWDER

2 ounces salt pork, diced
2 tablespoons finely chopped green pepper
2 tablespoons finely chopped celery
1 small onion, minced
5 cups milk
2 cups light cream
2 10-ounce packages frozen whole-kernel corn, thawed
1½ cups boiled potatoes, diced
½ teaspoon salt
freshly ground pepper

In large pot fry pork, stirring often, until browned. Remove browned pork fat and lower heat under pot. Add green pepper, celery and onion. Cook for 4 or 5 minutes, stirring. Add milk and cream and bring to a boil. Reduce heat, add corn, potatoes, salt and pepper. Cook for 8 minutes.

Serves 6.

LADY CURZON SOUP

Practically instant, this soup provides a spectacular effect, as well as an unusual flavor.

1 can split pea soup
1 can clear turtle soup
½ cup water
1 tablespoon sherry
1 teaspoon curry powder
½ cup heavy cream

Combine split pea and turtle soup, water, sherry and curry powder in saucepan. Stir and heat thoroughly. Ladle into oven-proof soup bowls or cups and place on cookie sheet. Spoon 2 tablespoons of lightly whipped heavy cream on top of each bowl of soup and place under broiler. When cream starts to brown, remove and serve immediately.

Serves 4.

MR. X's SOUP SAN MIGUEL

The gentleman who gave me this exquisite recipe said if his family ever found out he had divulged the formula, they'd never speak to him again.

> 2 10½-ounce cans beef consomme
> 1 cup walnuts, ground
> 1 cup heavy cream
> pinch nutmeg
> salt and pepper to taste

Bring consomme to a boil. Stir in walnuts and heavy cream. Heat, but don't boil. Add nutmeg and season with salt and pepper.

> *Serves 4 to 6.*

COLD PIMENTO SOUP

In the summertime, cold soup is always a pleasurable beginning to any meal. Most cooks stick with the expected gazpacho or vichyssoise. So, to be different, you might try cold pimento soup and it will quickly be added to your cold soup repertoire.

> 2 7-ounce cans pimentos, drained
> 2 cups chicken stock
> 2 cups tomato juice
> juice of 1 lemon
> 1 teaspoon Worcestershire sauce
> dash of Tabasco sauce
> salt and freshly ground pepper to taste

Puree ingredients in blender until smooth. Chill soup for several hours.

Garnish with chopped scallions and croutons.

> *Serves 4 to 6.*

GAZPACHO

This refreshing soup is pure nectar on a hot summer's day. Have friends join in the vegetable chopping and enjoy the result together.

> 4 large ripe tomatoes, chopped
> 2 medium cucumbers, peeled and chopped
> 1 green pepper, seeded and chopped
> 2 cloves garlic, peeled and chopped
> 1 red onion, chopped
> ¼ cup red wine vinegar
> ½ teaspoon dried basil
> 3 tablespoons olive oil
> 2 teaspoons salt
> 2 cups tomato juice
> 2 cups beef stock
> dash or two of Tabasco sauce
> garnishes

Combine ingredients in large bowl. Puree in blender a few cupfuls at a time. Pour pureed soup into clean container, adjust seasoning and chill thoroughly. Serve in soup tureen or large attractive bowl.

Place little bowls of the following garnishes around tureen: diced green pepper, diced cucumber, diced red onion, fried croutons, diced celery and diced tomato.

> Serves 6.

VICHYSSOISE

> 3 tablespoons butter
> 3 leeks, cleaned and sliced (white parts only)
> 2 tablespoons chopped yellow onion
> 2 potatoes, peeled and diced
> 4 cups chicken broth
> 1 cup heavy cream
> salt and white pepper to taste
> fresh chopped chives

Heat butter in saucepan and saute leeks and onion over medium heat for about 5 minutes, stirring often. Add potatoes and broth, bring to a boil. Reduce heat and simmer for 30 minutes. Puree 2 cups at a time in blender or food mill. Return to saucepan; add cream and season to taste with salt and pepper. Let cool at room temperature, cover and refrigerate for several hours.

Garnish with fresh chopped chives.

Serves 4.

DANIEL LABEILLE'S CREME "SOUFFLÉ D'ÉTÉ"

Daniel Labeille from Skaneateles, New York, teaches drama and, occasionally, gourmet cooking. His savory soup wins applause whenever it's served. According to Mr. Labeille, "The soup described below was arrived at quite accidentally on a very humid summer day. I have always regarded cucumbers as a very refreshing but sometimes indigestible ingredient. This cold soup recipe, because of the seeding and the cooking, manages to accentuate the more attractive qualities of this readily available vegetable."

> 2 large fresh cucumbers
> 1 large yellow onion
> 1 fresh sweet red pepper (small can of roasted, not pickled, pimentoes may be substituted)
> 2 tablespoons butter
> 2½ cups chicken broth, fresh or very good quality canned
> 1 teaspoon salt
> ¼ teaspoon dried tarragon (or 1 teaspoon fresh tarragon)
> ½ pint fresh heavy cream
> Tabasco sauce to taste (a dash or two)
> juice of 1 lemon
> freshly ground white pepper
> chopped chives

Trim ends off and peel cucumbers. Cut in half lengthwise and scoop out seeds with a teaspoon. Cut cucumbers into 1-inch chunks and set aside. Peel onion, cut in half and slice thin. Trim end off pepper, seed and cut into small pieces. In a large saucepan melt the butter and cook onion to soften but not brown. Then add cucumbers and red pepper, chicken broth, salt and tarragon. Bring to a boil. Reduce heat and simmer for 20 minutes. Remove from heat and strain solids, reserving liquid. Puree solids in food processor, blender, or food mill. Return pureed solids to liquid. Allow to cool and refrigerate till very cold. Whip fresh cream till moderately stiff. Incorporate whipped cream into soup base with wire whisk. Adjust seasoning to taste with Tabasco sauce, lemon juice, additional salt, and freshly ground white pepper. Serve in chilled bowls and top with chopped chives.

Serves 4.

chapter 3 · egg dishes

Eggs are a definite boon to the busy cook. Eggs can be poached, shirred or baked, served as omelets, in quiches or as frittatas. They are used as thickening agents in sauces and are a necessity in most cakes and breads. For an elegant touch, try a fried or poached egg on top of breaded veal, sliced roast beef, a hamburger or corned beef hash. Eggs cooked by themselves must be timed carefully and proper heat is crucial—as you know if you have ever found yourself serving eggs with burned white edges and broken yolks. If the frying pan for your eggs is seasoned* and well-buttered or oiled, the eggs should cook quickly and easily over a medium-high heat. To make perfect sunnyside-up eggs, cover the pan. The heat saved bounces back and helps cook the top of the egg slightly. When turning an egg, do it quickly but gently with a spatula. If you don't have a well-seasoned pan, get a Teflon one—either will prevent eggs from sticking to them.

ALFRED DRAKE'S LIGURIAN FRITTATA
(Courtesy of his ancestors)

When I asked Alfred, the actor/singer, for a recipe, this is what he sent me:

Frittata: *Omelette. (Cambridge Italian dictionary)*

Omelet: *A dish consisting of eggs, whipped up, seasoned, and fried; often varied by the addition of other ingredients. (Oxford English dictionary)*

> A frittata is an omelet,
> Of that there is no doubt;
> What's in it varies greatly,
> But eggs are never out.
> It may be light and fluffy
> Like mousse-clouds in the sky,
> Or sturdy, thick and heavy
> And rather like a pie.
> My Grandma taught my mother,
> My Mother then taught me
> Liguria's special version,

* The seasoned pan is discussed under omelets in this section.

Just try it and you'll see:
It's dandy hot or cold
No matter how you eat it.
Try various ingredients,
You simply cannot beat it.

5 tablespoons vegetable oil
2 tablespoons finely chopped onion
¾ cup green peas
1 fresh zucchini, cleaned, ends trimmed off and shred-
    ded (or 1 cup of shredded lettuce)*
1 tablespoon freshly chopped parsley
½ teaspoon dried basil
6 eggs
salt and freshly ground pepper to taste
2 tablespoons freshly grated Parmesan cheese

Heat 2 tablespoons oil and cook onion for 3 or 4 minutes until transparent. Add green peas, zucchini, parsley and basil. Cook for 5 minutes over low heat, stirring gently. Transfer to colander lined with paper towels and drain. In a 9- to 10-inch skillet with curved sides, heat 3 tablespoons oil. Combine eggs with salt, pepper and cheese. Pour eggs into pan and stir. Add vegetables and stir to combine with eggs, cooking over low heat. Lift edges of frittata with spatula and allow uncooked egg to run underneath. When eggs are set, shake pan until frittata slides freely in pan. Hold frittata in place with back of spatula and carefully pour off excess oil and reserve. Gently slide frittata onto a plate. Add reserved oil to pan. Cover frittata on plate with flat pan lid which fits skillet and invert. Slide frittata back into pan. Cook for just a minute or two and remove to heated serving dish. Cut into wedges.

Serves 4.

I answered Alfred with:

This Italian recipe
Is fine at cocktail time
Or cold for a late supper—
Just add a little lime.

* Almost any leftover vegetable will serve the same purpose.

TO POACH AN EGG

1 teaspoon white vinegar
1 raw egg or as many as you need

Fill a frying pan to a depth of 1½ inches of water, and bring to a boil. Add vinegar and reduce heat to a simmer. Break egg into saucer and slide gently into water. Cook for 3 or 4 minutes, until white is set. Carefully remove with a slotted spoon or a skimmer. Drain the eggs on paper towels and trim off uneven edges. If not using eggs immediately, they can be kept in large bowl of iced water. When ready to use, plunge into hot water for a moment.

KIPPERS AND SCRAMBLED EGGS

4 kippers, skinned and boned (can be purchased canned)
4 eggs
salt and pepper
2 tablespoons butter

Break cleaned kippers into small pieces and place in small bowl until ready to use. Beat eggs and season lightly with salt and pepper. Since kippers are very salty, little salt is needed, if any. Melt butter in skillet and when foaming subsides, add eggs and stir with wooden spoon. As eggs are starting to solidify, add kipper flakes. Stir with wooden spoon until eggs are done.

Serve with hot buttered toast.

Serves 2.

EGGS BENEDICT FOR TWO

I have always considered Eggs Benedict a romantic late-night or brunch dish. It is excellent served with chilled champagne.

1 cup Hollandaise Sauce (See index for recipe)
4 slices baked ham
2 tablespoons butter
4 poached eggs
1 teaspoon white vinegar
2 English muffins, halved
4 slices truffle or black olive or paprika

Prepare Hollandaise Sauce and place in container in bowl of warm water to keep hot. Saute ham on both sides in butter in skillet. Meanwhile, poach eggs: In large skillet place 1½ inches water plus 1 teaspoon white vinegar, and bring to a boil; reduce heat to a simmer. Gently drop 4 eggs into 4 different spots in water. Cook for 3 or 4 minutes until eggs are just set. Remove with slotted spoon and drain. Toast English muffins and place piece of ham on each half. Top each with a poached egg and spoon Hollandaise Sauce over top. Garnish with a slice of truffle or olive, or sprinkle with paprika.

Serves 2.

BASIC OMELET

2 tablespoons butter
3 eggs
salt and pepper to taste
freshly chopped parsley

Heat butter in an omelet pan or skillet with sloping sides and a bottom diameter of 8 inches. Season eggs with salt and pepper and mix with fork for 15 seconds. Pour eggs into pan and, using fork, immediately stir eggs in a circular motion. As eggs begin to set, smooth with back of the fork. With large spoon or spatula, begin turning omelet over in pan while tilting pan slightly to one side. Turn onto hot plate. Sprinkle with parsley.

HERB OMELET:

Add ¼ teaspoon dried tarragon and a pinch of dried basil to eggs before cooking them. Proceed as in recipe for basic omelet.

CHEESE OMELET:

Add 1 ounce grated cheese (Swiss, Cheddar or American) to basic omelet recipe before cooking eggs.

MUSHROOM OMELET:

Slice 3 fresh mushrooms thin and saute in 1 tablespoon of butter in small skillet for 4 minutes. Make omelet and before turning it, add mushrooms to middle of eggs; then fold omelet over.

WESTERN OMELET:

Saute 1 tablespoon chopped green pepper, 1 teaspoon chopped onion and 2 tablespoons chopped ham for 5 minutes in 1 tablespoon butter in small skillet. Add to basic omelet recipe and prepare omelet.

To Season an Omelet Pan

In order to make a successful omelet the pan must be properly seasoned to allow the eggs to slide in the pan. The best type of pan for making an omelet is a French iron pan with sloping sides, about 7 to 8 inches in diameter. To season this pan, first scrub it well with scouring pad and powder or soap. Dry pan well and rub it with vegetable oil. Let it rest for several hours. Then sprinkle liberally with salt, heat and rub it with crumpled paper towels until clean. Pan is ready to use. When pan has been used, wipe it out with paper towels. Washing isn't necessary. Season pan with oil and salt in the above described method if pan sticks next time you use it. If possible use this pan only for omelets.

WILLIAM E. BURROWS' LOBSTER AND CHEESE OMELET

William E. Burrows, who is Associate Professor of Journalism at New York University and author of Vigilante!, *elucidates: "Back in the days when you didn't have to pawn your great aunt's harpsichord to get lobster and smoked salmon, I used to prepare two egg dishes which were especially popular for Sunday brunch. (The last time we did the annual Washington Square Black Squirrel Count, I prepared both, but civil rights protesters and inflation ended that forever.)*

"My secret is singing to whatever dish I'm preparing—no easy feat when you compose the songs yourself. My standards include 'Go on Lamb when you Get a Bum Steer,' 'Dancing Beak to Beak,' and, for eggs, 'Chol Es Terol' (Loosely translated from an early Portuguese fado: 'A good woman will break your yolk, but she'll never break your heart.')"

> 2½ tablespoons butter
> 1 7-ounce can lobster meat
> 1 scallion, finely chopped
> ¼ teaspoon dried tarragon
> 4 eggs, lightly beaten
> 2 slices Muenster cheese, shredded
> salt and pepper to taste
> freshly chopped parsley

Heat 1 tablespoon butter in small skillet. Saute lobster, scallion and tarragon, stirring occasionally, for 2 minutes and set aside. Heat 1½ tablespoons butter in 10-inch skillet with curved sides, making sure butter covers bottom and sides of pan. Add beaten eggs, seasoned with salt and pepper, and stir with fork for a few seconds until eggs just begin to set. Spread eggs evenly over pan and place lobster mixture on half of surface. Cover with cheese. With large spoon begin lifting empty side of omelet and turn over on top of eggs. Tilt pan toward you at an angle. When eggs seem set, place pan near heated serving plate and turn omelet gently into plate. Sprinkle with freshly chopped parsley. Divide in half and put one half of omelet on another warmed plate.

Serves 2.

WILLIAM E. BURROWS' LOX 'N EGGS

2 tablespoons butter
1 small onion, sliced
4 eggs, beaten
salt and pepper to taste
¼ pound Nova Scotia salmon, thinly sliced

Heat butter in skillet and saute onion for 3 minutes, stirring occasionally. Add beaten eggs, seasoned with salt and pepper. Stir for a few seconds until they begin to set. Sprinkle salmon pieces over eggs and gently turn with large spoon until the eggs are cooked to your liking.

Serve with toasted bagels, cream cheese and Bloody Marys.

Serves 2.

QUICHE LORRAINE

6 to 8 strips cooked crisp bacon, crumbled
½ cup Swiss cheese, grated
2 tablespoons grated onion
3 eggs, beaten
1¾ cups light cream
dash nutmeg
¼ teaspoon salt
freshly ground pepper to taste
9-inch unbaked pie shell (See index for recipe)

Arrange bacon pieces across bottom of pie shell. Sprinkle with cheese and onion. Put eggs, cream, nutmeg, salt and pepper in bowl and beat. Pour over cheese and bacon. Bake in preheated 375 F. oven for about 40 minutes, until browned on top and puffy.

Serves 6.

chapter 4. sauces

BÉCHAMEL SAUCE

4 tablespoons butter
4 tablespoons flour
2 cups milk
salt and white pepper to taste

Melt butter in heavy saucepan. With a wire whisk, stir in flour over medium heat. Continue stirring mixture after it begins to bubble for one minute. (This cooks the flour and eliminates the raw flavor.) Slowly pour in milk, constantly stirring. The mixture at first will be lumpy, but as you stir and beat, it will become smooth and thicken. When sauce reaches a boil, reduce heat and cook, stirring, for about 2 minutes. Season well with salt and pepper.

For creamier sauce, replace ½ cup of milk with light or heavy cream at the end with the salt and pepper.

Yield: about 2 cups.

MORNAY SAUCE

To make Mornay Sauce, use ½ cup of cream in preceding Béchamel recipe and stir in ½ cup shredded Swiss or Cheddar cheese with the salt and pepper, stirring until the cheese melts.

A stronger Mornay Sauce can be made by adding ¼ cup grated Parmesan cheese to sauce with other cheese as described above.

Yield: about 2¼ cups.

CURRY SAUCE

1½ cups mayonnaise
2 tablespoons lemon juice
2 teaspoons curry powder
pinch cayenne pepper
1 tablespoon minced green pepper
1 tablespoon minced scallions

Mix together thoroughly.

Yield: 1½ cups.

HOLLANDAISE SAUCE

This heavenly sauce is not difficult to prepare, but it can be tricky because the egg yolks can curdle quickly if overheated. Follow directions carefully and you should have perfect results.

> *4 egg yolks*
> *1 tablespoon lemon juice*
> *1 tablespoon cold water*
> *pinch cayenne pepper*
> *1½ sticks (6 ounces) butter*

Put water into the bottom pan of a double boiler, but make sure it doesn't touch the bottom of the top pan. Bring water to a boil, reduce heat to a simmer. In top pan place egg yolks and beat for 1 minute with wire whisk. Add lemon juice, water and cayenne pepper. Place pan over simmering water and add 1 tablespoon butter and stir with whisk until sauce begins to thicken. Add remaining butter a tablespoon at a time until each is incorporated into sauce. If at any point sauce begins to form lumps, immediately remove from heat and lower bottom of pan into pan of cold water, constantly stirring to cool mixture. Serve immediately or place pan in another pan of warm water and sauce will keep for about 1 hour.

> *Yield: 1 cup.*

BÉARNAISE SAUCE

> *2 tablespoons finely chopped shallots*
> *3 tablespoons white wine vinegar*
> *¼ cup dry white wine or dry vermouth*
> *½ tablespoon dried tarragon*
> *1 teaspoon fresh chopped parsley*

Place shallots, vinegar, vermouth and tarragon in small, heavy saucepan and bring to a boil. Cook over medium high heat until liquid in pan is reduced to 2 tablespoons. Pour into small bowl to cool. Meanwhile, prepare Hollandaise Sauce in preceding recipe, eliminating lemon juice and water. Add cooled wine mixture to egg yolks (strain if desired) and continue making sauce. Check seasoning and add 1 teaspoon fresh chopped parsley.

Yield: 1 cup.

SAUCE MOUSSELINE

This is a lighter sauce usually served with fish or vegetables such as asparagus or broccoli. It is made by folding ½ cup of heavy cream which has been whipped into 1 cup Hollandaise Sauce.

Yield: about 2 cups.

MUSTARD SAUCE

⅓ cup vegetable oil
2 tablespoons Dijon-style mustard
2 tablespoons heavy cream
1 teaspoon fresh chopped parsley
salt and pepper to taste

Whisk ingredients together and serve on vegetable or salad.

Yield: About ¾ cup.

THICK MUSTARD SAUCE FOR CHOPPED STEAK

¼ cup prepared mustard, Dijon preferred
¼ cup ketchup
1 tablespoon finely chopped onion
½ teaspoon Worcestershire sauce
¼ teaspoon soy sauce

Combine ingredients and serve with chopped meat.

Yield: About ½ cup.

RÉMOULADE SAUCE

1½ cups mayonnaise
⅓ cup minced dill pickle
2 hard-boiled eggs, chopped
2 teaspoons prepared mustard
1 tablespoon capers
1 teaspoon fresh chopped parsley

Combine all ingredients.

Yield: about 1½ cups.

VERY EASY MUSHROOM SAUCE

This sauce is so delicious it can be served on toast, but it is a flavor enhancer for broiled or poached fish, sauteed or roast chicken or veal. And it's not bad on a grilled steak, either.

4 tablespoons butter
⅓ pound fresh mushrooms, finely chopped
⅓ cup dry white wine
½ cup chicken stock
1 teaspoon lemon juice
¾ cup heavy cream
1 scant tablespoon cornstarch or arrowroot
salt and freshly ground pepper to taste

Melt butter in medium-size saucepan. Add mushrooms, stir, cover and simmer for about 4 minutes. Add wine, chicken stock and lemon juice. Stir, re-cover and simmer for 5 minutes. Add cream, bring to a boil and cook for 3 minutes. Dissolve cornstarch or arrowroot in a little chicken stock and add to sauce. Stir until sauce has thickened nicely. Season well with salt and pepper.

Yield: about 2½ cups.

HOMEMADE MAYONNAISE

About ten minutes and the strength of a beating arm produces classic homemade mayonnaise. Once experienced you're not likely to settle for a commercial brand.

> *2 large egg yolks, at room temperature*
> *½ teaspoon dry mustard*
> *½ teaspoon salt*
> *dash cayenne pepper*
> *2 tablespoons lemon juice or white wine vinegar*
> *1½ cups vegetable or olive oil (olive oil makes a more*
> *   potent sauce)*
> *1 tablespoon boiling water*

Beat egg yolks in mixing bowl with wire whisk for a minute or two. Add dry mustard, salt, cayenne pepper and 1 tablespoon lemon juice. Beat about 40 strokes. Now the oil may be added, *a drop at a time* (so that the yolks can absorb the oil), until all oil is used and sauce has thickened. Never stop beating. Beat in remaining lemon juice and the boiling water into mayonnaise and check seasoning.

> *Yield: about 2 cups.*

TARTAR SAUCE

> *1 cup mayonnaise*
> *1 tablespoon chopped capers*
> *1 tablespoon chopped sweet pickles*
> *1 tablespoon fresh chopped parsley*
> *2 teaspoons vinegar*
> *1 tablespoon grated onion*

Combine ingredients and refrigerate for several hours before serving.

> *Yield: about 1½ cups.*

chapter 5. vegetables

Vegetables are rich in vitamins and minerals, low in calories, beautiful to the eye, inexpensive and delicious if prepared with imagination. What more could one ask? In the spring and summer, when fresh truck-farm vegetables are plentiful (or if you're lucky, those from your own garden), I often serve a meal that consists of three or four cooked vegetables with fresh baked bread, and no meat at all.

The simplest way to cook vegetables is to steam them. It is also the best way to preserve the flavor of fresh, crisp vegetables. Cover the bottom of a large pot or steamer with an inch or so of water, and place the vegetables in the steamer tray or any device with a perforated bottom that can be raised above the water. This allows the steam from the boiling water to rise and cook the vegetables. Cooking time is slightly longer than for boiling vegetables, but test for your own taste in crispness.

JACQUES PÉPIN'S CREPES DE MAIS

Jacques Pepin was born in Lyons, the capital of French gastronomy, and began training in a restaurant kitchen at thirteen years of age. He's worked in many of the finest French restaurants in France and the United States, including the Pavillon, and he was once chef to Charles de Gaulle. He's written many cookbooks and articles on food and has taught thousands of students the joys of French cooking. I've studied with him and worked alongside him at the New York Times Cooking School. He has a remarkable talent for teaching and illustrating cooking techniques with good humor, spirit and endless energy. I'm forever grateful for all he has taught me, and for his friendship.

Jacques says, "The best ingredients for cooking are knowledge and getting involved." He insists that his students do the work, while he demonstrates only sophisticated or complicated methods. While he's a classicist, he is in no way rigid when it comes to saving time with a food processor or blending certain food with an electric mixer.

He eagerly urges people to be inventive and create new dishes and the corn crepe recipe he's given me for this book is one he originated with inspiration from his wife Gloria.

> 5 medium-size ears of corn, husked and silk removed
> 4 tablespoons flour
> 4 eggs
> 1 teaspoon salt
> ¼ teaspoon freshly ground pepper
> ½ cup heavy cream
> ½ stick (¼ cup) sweet butter, melted

Bring a pot of salted water to a rolling boil. Drop the husked, cleaned corn into the water and let come to a boil again. Remove corn from water immediately, and let cool until it can be handled. With a sharp knife, cut straight down the middle of each kernel row, slitting each kernel open. Then hold the ear in one hand, the top of the ear resting on the table, and, with a spoon, scrape the pulp out of the opened kernels, extracting all of it as you scrape down the full length of the ear, and all around the ear, row by row. The skin of the kernels that held the pulp will remain attached to the ear; the pulp will be removed. You will have about 1¼ cups of pulp.

Put the pulp in a large bowl and sprinkle with the flour. Mix well with a whisk. Add the eggs, salt and pepper, mixing to blend all ingredients well. Add the cream and combine well. Finally, add the melted butter and mix together once more. Heat oven to 180 F. Place a crepe pan or seasoned heavy iron pan over low to medium heat. When pan is hot, pour 2 tablespoons of the mixture into the pan. This amount is enough for one crepe. If the skillet is large enough to hold two crepes, make two at a time, otherwise use several pans. Each crepe should be about 4 inches in diameter. Cook 40 seconds on one side; flip over or turn with a large spatula, and cook 30 seconds on the other side. Keep the finished crepes hot in oven while you are making the others. Makes about 20 crepes to serve as a first course or with beef, veal or rabbit stews.

> Serves 6.

BOILED ASPARAGUS

If I had to pick a vegetable that I'd be willing to eat every day for the rest of my life, it would be asparagus. Elegant asparagus is a good first course or side dish. When buying asparagus select firm stalks with closed tips. It doesn't matter whether you use thin or heavy stalks; they are both tender. The heavier stalks, of course, take less time to peel. Six heavy stalks are plenty to serve as a first course.

> 2 pounds asparagus
> ½ teaspoon salt

With small, sharp knife, shallowly pare off outer skin, beginning at bottom of stalk, until you near top of stalk. Wash pared asparagus under cold slow-running water and drain. Asparagus can be tied in 3 inch bundles, but this isn't necessary. Bring water to boil in pan large enough to hold asparagus. Add salt. Lower asparagus into water to cover and bring to a rolling boil again. Reduce heat to low boil and cook asparagus for 10 minutes. Test for doneness by piercing bottom of stalk with sharp point of knife. If it is tender to the touch, asparagus is ready. (Never overcook asparagus or any other vegetable.) Carefully remove asparagus with serving forks and drain.

> Serves 4 to 6.

Asparagus can be served hot with Hollandaise or a sauce of lemon and butter or cold with a Vinaigrette or Mustard Sauce. (See index for recipes.)

Special Note:
Raw asparagus with a good dip is delicious as an appetizer. I like it with a mild Curry Sauce Dip.

CURRY SAUCE DIP:

> 1 cup mayonnaise
> juice of 1 lemon
> 1 teaspoon curry powder

Combine sauce thoroughly and chill for several hours before serving.

BOILED ARTICHOKES

A cold artichoke with a Vinaigrette Sauce is an excellent first course. I remember serving them to a date at dinner and, in the midst of lively conversation, I realized my friend had tackled half the artichoke leaves and was eating the wrong ends. We had a good laugh. If you're just learning about the glorious globe, here are the full instructions.

> *4 artichokes*
> *1 lemon*
> *1 teaspoon salt*

Cut off stem of artichoke at its base. Pull off a few small leaves so artichoke will stand up straight. Cut off top of center of artichoke and trim off points of each leaf with a pair of scissors. Place artichokes in colander and run cold water over them. Rub each cut part with lemon halves. Drop artichokes into salted boiling water which covers them and cook for about 45 minutes. The cooking time will depend on their size. Forty-five minutes is for a large artichoke. The artichokes are done when leaves pull off easily and bottoms are tender to the point of a knife. Drain cooked artichokes in collander upside down. They may be served immediately while hot or refrigerated and served cold. Serve with Hollandaise or melted butter when hot or a Vinaigrette Sauce or favorite dressing if cold. (See index for recipes.)

Eating instructions:

Pull off a leaf from the bottom with your fingers and dip it in sauce, then eat the end you are not touching with your fingers. As you finish eating tender part of leaves, place the rest in the saucer under the artichoke dish or in the extra plate provided for this purpose. After you've finished the leaves and come to the top, take a knife and fork and gently cut away hairy center. You've reached the heart of the artichoke, the best part. Cut into pieces with your fork and knife and savor.

GREEN BEANS WITH BACON AND TOMATOES

¼ pound slab bacon
2 10-ounce packages frozen green beans
2 tablespoons oil
1 medium-large onion, chopped
2 cloves garlic, crushed
1 8-ounce can whole tomatoes, chopped
¼ teaspoon dried thyme
1 tablespoon fresh chopped parsley
¼ teaspoon salt
freshly ground pepper to taste

Cut bacon into ½-inch cubes. Fry until crisp and reserve 1 teaspoon bacon drippings. Drain bacon on paper towels. Cook green beans according to package directions and drain. Meanwhile, add bacon drippings and oil to skillet and heat. Add onion and garlic. Cook over low heat, stirring occasionally, for 15 minutes. Add chopped tomatoes and liquid from can, bacon, cooked green beans, thyme, parsley, salt and pepper. Stir and simmer for about 5 minutes until thoroughly heated.

Serves 6.

FRIED PEPPERS AND ONIONS

2 large green bell peppers
2 large red peppers
¼ cup olive oil
1 medium-large onion, sliced
1 large clove garlic, minced
¼ teaspoon dried basil
¼ teaspoon dried oregano
salt and freshly ground pepper to taste

Remove stems from peppers and seed. Slice into 1-inch strips. Heat oil in large skillet, add peppers and remaining ingredients. Fry over medium heat, stirring, for about 5 minutes. Reduce heat to low, cover and cook 15 minutes.

Serve hot or cold.

Serves 4 to 6.

CORN ON THE COB

6 ears corn, husked
½ teaspoon sugar
1 teaspoon salt
½ cup milk

Bring enough water to cover corn to a boil. Add sugar, salt, milk and corn. Return to a boil; reduce heat and simmer for 5 minutes. Turn off heat and let corn rest in water for 2 minutes. Serve with salt, freshly ground pepper and plenty of butter.

Serves 3 to 4.

CREAMED SPINACH

2 pounds fresh spinach, stems removed and washed
2½ cups water
½ teaspoon salt
2 tablespoons butter
2 dashes nutmeg
¼ cup sour cream
¼ cup heavy cream
salt and freshly ground pepper to taste

Bring water seasoned with salt to a boil. Add spinach, cover and cook over medium heat for 5 minutes. Drain in colander. Press spinach with the back of a large spoon to get rid of most of water. Place spinach on chopping block and chop in 5 or 6 places. Do not chop finely. Melt butter in saucepan. Add spinach, nutmeg, sour and heavy cream and stir until blended. Cover and cook over low heat for 4 or 5 minutes. Season with salt and pepper.

Serves 4.

JOHN EHLE'S WILD MUSHROOMS À LA CRÈME

John Ehle is the author of eight novels and four works of non-fiction including a marvelous study entitled, **The Cheeses and Wines of England and France with Notes on Irish Whiskey.** *He is married to the actress Rosemary Harris. They live in North Carolina with daughter Jennifer. I am delighted he shares his knowledge of the art of wild mushroom hunting and preparation with us in this book:*

At a fishing camp some years ago, in the valley just below Mount Mitchell, I had the opportunity to go wild mushroom hunting with one or the other of two nationally recognized authorities. I made my choice, and for three delightful hours watched him pick and choose and reject and ruminate. We closed out the day with two baskets full of colorful, pungent specimens. When we returned to the lodge, the other expert was waiting there with his discoveries, and there ensued a heated argument between the men as they debated the identities of their finds. I soon realized that the dangers of eating wild mushrooms do not lie exclusively with the mushrooms.

Since then I have bought my own basket. Into it I confidently place those specimens I know well, and no others: morels in spring (one of the Lord's best formed phallic symbols, appearing briefly under old apple trees, and other places), the chantrelle (a small horn of plenty growing out of shaded earth, the color of an egg yolk when the yolk is cooked hard), the green russula (the only mushroom I know that has a mottled green cap), and several boleti, the most plentiful and enduring, the easiest to identify, the safest of all. Boleti are the mushrooms that have an underside to the cap which looks like foam rubber. Actually this foamy mass is the collection of tubes from whose exposed, open ends come the reproductive spores.

Only a few of the many different species of boleti are poisonous—that is, will make the eater nauseated for a few hours. None of them is deadly. To be able to discard the poisonous ones, observe these two rules which have served my friends and me well in Western North Carolina: discard the mushroom if the tube end, the foam-rubber bottom, is reddish colored, or if when bruised or broken the foam-rubber bottom changes color. Usually the change will be to blue or greenish blue and requires only a few seconds. Of course, you will discard far more eatable ones than poisonous ones, but all rules are wasteful, which is one of their charms.

My favorite boleti is the edulis, the famous cèpe of the French. Its *cap, which is four to six inches across, is pale brown in youth, becoming reddish brown, and finally tawny brown. Its tubes, white at first, become creamy yellow and finally might turn greenish. It is a hefty, fleshy, royal mushroom which springs up in the same location year after year, as do all boleti, under oaks and pines, in woods and along the borders of woods as well as in the open, even on the front lawn of my mountain house at Penland, appearing there in July.*

I also like the pictus. Its cap is carmine colored and later becomes spotted with red, its tubes are pale yellow and darken with age. It grows mostly under white pines, or so I find it, and spans the summer months, and will even continue to poke its beautiful heads above ground until frost during rainy autumns.

There are several others which we enjoy eating: the Americanus, bright yellow caps, the granulatus and the luteus, both of which become so viscid, even glutinous in wet weather that pine needles cling tenaciously to their caps, so that it's best to peel the skin off the cap. You will want to pick different kinds—carry a mushroom guidebook with you the first few hunts.

A few boleti are bitter, so until you know the ones you can trust, you might nibble at the edges of strangers.

As you pick each mushroom, break or cut off its dirty foot. At home, brush off the mushrooms. Never wash, do not even rinse any mushroom. Separate the caps from the stems. Peel off and discard the foam-rubber bottom if it appears to be past its prime or soggy.

When you are ready to cook them, halve or quarter the largest caps, slice the tender and healthy part of the stem into quarter-inch-thick rounds. Heat butter (approximately 1½ tablespoons per ½ pound mushrooms) until it begins to change color, and fry the mushrooms without crowding them for two or three minutes, maybe longer if you want them to begin to be crisp. They are about eighty per cent water and do not accept crispness naturally. Sprinkle salt on them. Please agree not to add mace, ginger, sassafras, thyme, oregano, curry or any other infernal distraction. A cèpe or pictus does not need to be improved, and its mild flavor can easily be buried.

For variation, you might—after frying ½ pound mushrooms in 1½ tablespoons of butter—pour ⅓ pint of cream into the skillet. Stew the cream, without letting it boil, until the sauce thickens, which it will on its own without addition of flour or other thickeners. Serve the mushrooms in the steaming sauce. (Incidentally, you can pour the mushrooms and this cream and butter sauce into containers, plop them into a freezer, and serve them whenever you need them, even ten months later in my experience, by heating them up, then adding a teaspoon of fresh butter. I have found this the best way to preserve the taste of boleti, chantrelles, even morels.)

Wild mushrooms ought to be served in small quantities, even though you might at that very moment know of places where bushels of them are being left unpicked. They are a delicacy, and ought to be respected as such. We must protect ourselves from our occasional greed and nature's occasional abundance, if we are to remain in awe of these wild creations year after year.

SAUTEED MUSHROOMS

Mushrooms are an elegant side dish for any meat, fowl or seafood meal. This recipe is quick, simple and has a zingy flavor.

> *4 strips bacon*
> *4 tablespoons butter*
> *¾ pound mushrooms, thinly sliced*
> *1 large clove garlic, finely chopped*
> *1 teaspoon lemon juice*
> *1 tablespoon dried bread crumbs*
> *salt and freshly ground pepper to taste*
> *fresh chopped parsley*

Cook bacon in large skillet until crisp. Remove bacon, drain and crumble. Place bacon in small bowl until ready to use. Pour out all but 1 tablespoon bacon fat from skillet, add butter and melt. Add mushrooms and saute for 5 minutes, turning a few times. Add garlic, lemon juice, bread crumbs, salt, pepper and bacon, then gently turn. Cook over medium high heat for 3 or 4 minutes and transfer to serving dish.

Sprinkle with parsley.

> *Serves 4 to 6.*

CREAMED ONIONS AU GRATIN

16 small white onions
4 tablespoons butter
3 tablespoons flour
1½ cups milk, scalded
½ teaspoon salt
freshly ground pepper
bread crumbs
freshly chopped parsley

Trim ends off onions and boil in water to cover onions for about 20 minutes. Meanwhile, in saucepan melt butter, sprinkle with flour and stir with whisk until well blended. Slowly whisk in hot milk until sauce is smooth and thickens. Season with salt and pepper. Add cooked and drained onions to sauce, sprinkle top with crumbs, and thoroughly heat. Transfer to shallow baking dish and place under broiler until lightly browned on top.

Garnish with fresh chopped parsley.

Serves 4.

FRIED GREEN PLANTAINS

4 green plantains*
1 cup vegetable oil
salt

Peel plantains with sharp knife. Cut into 1½-inch lengths. Heat oil in skillet. Fry plantains on one end for 5 minutes, turn and fry on other end for 5 more minutes. Remove plantains and place on paper towels. Cover with several pieces of paper towel and, with the palm of your hand, press each plantain to flatten. Fry flattened patties a few pieces at a time until golden on each side. Add more oil, if necessary. Sprinkle with salt. Serve with black beans and rice or Arroz con Pollo.

Serves 6 to 8.

*Available in Spanish food shops

PUREED PEAS

2 cups chicken broth
2 10-ounce packages frozen green peas
2 tablespoons butter
3 tablespoons heavy cream

Pour chicken broth into saucepan and bring to a boil. Add peas and bring to a boil again. Reduce heat and cook for 5 minutes. Drain peas and reserve 2 tablespoons liquid. Place peas in food blender with 2 tablespoons cooking liquid, butter and heavy cream. Puree for 30 seconds.

Serves 6.

BAKED EGGPLANT WITH MOZZARELLA CRUST

1 large eggplant
4 tablespoons butter
1 small onion, finely chopped
½ cup bread crumbs
¼ teaspoon salt
freshly ground pepper to taste
¾ cup shredded mozzarella cheese

Cut eggplant in half and bake in preheated 375 F. oven for 35 minutes. Meanwhile, heat 2 tablespoons butter in small saucepan. Add chopped onion and cook, stirring, for 3 or 4 minutes. Add remaining butter. Stir in bread crumbs and cook over low heat for a minute. Remove from heat and set aside. When eggplant is tender, scoop out meat of eggplant and place in shallow baking dish and chop into small pieces. Stir in salt and pepper. Spread eggplant evenly over baking dish and sprinkle with bread crumb mixture. Top with mozzarella. Place in preheated oven at 375 F. and cook for 10 to 12 minutes or until top is golden.

Serves 4.

A SCOUNDREL'S RATATOUILLE

For a short time I dated a handsome and gracious Frenchman, who will remain nameless. He always wined and dined me in excellent restaurants. So I was quite nervous when I finally cooked him a French meal; but I succeeded in pleasing his palate. He admitted to being a rather competent cook himself, and boasted of a spectacular ratatouille he executed on rare occasions of importance, one of which was to be our next date.

His apartment was beautiful, at its center a sunken living room, and a dining room that was a large, tastefully appointed room, but wasn't set yet for dinner. My host handed me a tall, thin glass of champagne, asked me to join him for dinner, and guided me into the bedroom, where a splendid dinner was spread across his king-size bed. When I asked him why dinner was set up on the bed, he replied, "That's where the tablecloth is."

In the end, he agreed to placing chairs on either side of the bed for our meal, but protested that we were too far apart for dinner conversation. He was original in some ways, and I did get the ratatouille recipe from the rascal.

> ⅓ cup olive or vegetable oil
> 1 medium onion, chopped
> 2 cloves garlic, crushed
> 1 medium eggplant, peeled and cubed
> 1 large green pepper, seeded and chopped
> 3 tomatoes, peeled and chopped
> 2 medium zucchini, ends trimmed off, cut in half, then sliced
> 1 tablespoon fresh chopped parsley
> 1 teaspoon salt
> freshly ground pepper
> ½ cup water

Heat oil and saute onion and garlic for 5 minutes over low heat. Add remaining ingredients, stir several times, cover and simmer for 45 minutes. Stir occasionally.

Serves 6 to 8.

Cold ratatouille is an excellent picnic dish.

APPLESAUCE AND PINEAPPLE

Apples and pineapple are, of course, fruit, but I've included them in this section of the book to be considered as a side dish in place of vegetables.

> 1 10-ounce jar applesauce
> 1 8-ounce can crushed pineapple, drained
> dash of cinnamon
> 2 tablespoons butter

Place applesauce and pineapple in saucepan. Heat until mixture reaches the boiling point. Lower heat and add cinnamon and butter. Stir until butter melts.

Serve with pork or turkey.

> *Serves 4.*

POTATOES

Americans probably eat more potatoes than any other vegetable. Since potatoes can be prepared in a staggering number of ways, I'm always bewildered by the fact that they are usually served either fried or baked, in both restaurants and homes. Of course, fried or baked potatoes are good, but one tires of any food that's always cooked in the same manner.

Various kinds of potatoes differ chiefly in their starch content. The more starch in a potato the better it will be baked, mashed or fried. Boiling potatoes should have less starch so they won't fall apart when used in salads or pan-frying. The difference in potatoes across the country is great. To test potatoes, cook several kinds in boiling water and see which have a lot of starch (they'll fall apart easily). Generally speaking, the long Idaho potatoes are best for baking, frying or mashing, and round potatoes are best for boiling, pan-frying or salads.

When making potato salads be sure to add herbs, spices and seasonings while the potatoes are still hot so they will absorb the flavors. Potatoes are inexpensive, but add richly to menus. Try creating your own casserole with potatoes, your favorite vegetables and a cream sauce.

POTATOES VAN GOGH

My favorite artist is Vincent van Gogh. I celebrate his birthday every year on March 30th, and I have created a new dish in his honor. It was inspired by his extraordinary painting, *The Potato Eaters*.

> *12 boiling potatoes, peeled and shaped in uniform ovals*
> *½ cup shredded Cheddar cheese*
> *1 teaspoon finely chopped scallions*
> *2 tablespoons dry bread crumbs*
> *salt and pepper to taste*
> *3 tablespoons butter*

Boil potatoes in lightly salted water until tender. Arrange in buttered shallow baking dish. Combine cheese, scallions, bread crumbs, salt and pepper and sprinkle over potatoes. Dot with butter. Place under broiler until top is golden.

> *Serves 6.*

POMMES SAVONNETTE

> *2½ to 3 pounds boiling potatoes*
> *6 tablespoons butter*
> *salt and pepper*
> *1 teaspoon chopped parsley*

Cut the potatoes in ¾-inch thick slices across width. Peel each slice with small, sharp knife and bevel edges by cutting rim off both sides of slice. Put potatoes in cold water as they are trimmed. Drain potatoes and arrange in one layer on buttered au gratin dish or heavy aluminum skillet with metal handle. Add cold water to reach halfway up sides of potatoes. Season with salt and pepper. Dot with butter and bring to a boil on top of stove. Place in preheated 425 F. oven and bake for about 35 minutes. Water should have evaporated. Remove pan from oven and carefully turn potatoes with spatula. Bake for about 20 minutes more or until potatoes are golden on top. Remove to serving dish and sprinkle with chopped parsley.

> *Serves 6.*

GERMAN FRIES

1 pound Idaho potatoes, peeled
3 tablespoons butter
1 tablespoon oil
salt and pepper to taste

Slice potatoes about ⅛-inch thick and chop into 1-inch pieces.
Melt butter in large skillet and add oil. When hot, but not smoking, add potatoes and shake pan so that they evenly cover bottom
of pan. Cover and cook over medium low heat for about 12 minutes or until nicely browned. Turn potatoes with spatula, season
with salt and pepper, recover and cook until potatoes brown on
this side.

Serves 4.

POMMES ANNA

6 Idaho potatoes, peeled and thinly sliced
½ stick butter
salt and pepper to taste
parsley

Butter an 8-inch skillet with curved sides and metal handle. Place
a layer of potato slices slightly overlapping, in circles, flat on bottom and sides of pan. Dot with butter and sprinkle with salt and
pepper. Make another single layer of potatoes and dot with butter,
salt and pepper. Repeat this procedure until all potatoes are used.
Dot top with salt and pepper and press down lightly on potatoes
with a piece of buttered foil. Fit foil over skillet tightly and bake in
preheated 425 F. oven for about 35 minutes. Remove foil and press
potatoes down with spatula. Cook about 20 more minutes or until
potatoes are golden brown. Remove pan and allow potatoes to rest
for a few minutes. Shake pan to loosen bottom layer of potatoes.
Carefully use spatula if necessary. Using flat plate or lid over pan,
pour off excess butter. Invert pan over hot serving dish to remove
potatoes.
   Garnish center of potatoes with small cluster of fresh parsley.

Serves 6 to 8.

SAUTEED POTATOES WITH GARLIC

1 tablespoon butter
3 tablespoons vegetable oil
12 cloves garlic, unpeeled
4 Idaho potatoes, peeled and sliced thinly
salt and pepper to taste

In large skillet heat butter and oil. Over very low heat add garlic
cloves and push around with wooden spoon for 3 minutes. Place
potatoes in skillet and cook over medium low heat for 12 to 15
minutes until browned. Turn potatoes with large spatula and continue cooking until brown on all sides. Season well with salt and
pepper.

Serves 4 to 6.

GRATIN DAUPHINOIS
(French-Style Scalloped Potatoes)

8 to 10 medium-size boiling potatoes, peeled
1½ cups milk
½ cup heavy cream
2 tablespoons butter
1 teaspoon salt
freshly ground pepper
½ cup shredded Swiss or Cheddar cheese (optional)

Slice potatoes one at a time in food processor. Place potatoes in
buttered oval baking dish about 16 inches in length. Bring milk,
cream, and butter to a boil. Remove from heat and add salt. Pour
over potatoes. Sprinkle cheese over top, if used. Place on baking
sheet in preheated 375 F. oven and bake for 1 hour, until golden
on top.

Serves 8.

HASH BROWN POTATOES

6 medium potatoes, peeled and cut into ¾-inch cubes
2 tablespoons vegetable oil
2 tablespoons butter
1 medium onion, finely chopped
salt and freshly ground pepper to taste
parsley

In large saucepan heat enough lightly salted water to cover potatoes; boil them for 5 minutes. Drain well. Heat oil and butter in skillet, add potatoes and cook for 5 minutes and turn with spatula. Add onions and season with salt and pepper. Cook for 5 minutes and turn again. Cook until golden.
  Garnish with fresh chopped parsley.

Serves 6.

PERFECT BAKED POTATOES

4 Idaho potatoes, scrubbed
butter

Lightly rub each potato with butter. Pierce each one with fork tines. Place on oven rack in preheated 425 F. oven for about 45 minutes. Cooking time will depend on size of potato.
  Serve with butter or sour cream and chopped chives.

Serves 4.

HERB AND SOUR CREAM
STUFFED BAKED POTATOES

4 freshly baked potatoes
½ pint sour cream
½ teaspoon chopped chives
½ teaspoon dried tarragon
¼ teaspoon garlic powder
½ teaspoon salt or to taste
freshly ground pepper
¼ cup melted butter plus extra butter for basting

Cut potatoes in half and carefully scoop out pulp from halves without breaking potato skins. Mash pulp well and add remaining ingredients. Mix well and spoon mixture back into potato shells. Run fork tines along top of potato mounds to make ribbed design. Brush each potato with a little melted butter and place under broiler until golden.

Serves 4.

POTATO SALAD

6 medium potatoes, quartered
8 strips crisp cooked bacon, crumbled
1 medium onion, finely chopped
1/2 teaspoon chopped chives
2 stalks celery, finely chopped
2 hard-boiled eggs, chopped
1/3 cup white vinegar
1/2 cup mayonnaise
1 1/2 teaspoons prepared mustard
1/2 teaspoon salt or to taste
freshly ground pepper

Drop potatoes into boiling water to cover and bring to a boil again. Reduce heat to low boil and cook until tender, about 20 minutes. Don't overcook or potatoes will become mushy. Drain. While still hot, but cool enough to handle, peel and cut potatoes into slices and place in large bowl with remaining ingredients. Gently blend and chill a few hours before serving.

Serves 6.

LEGUMES
(Beans, Peas and Lentils)

Beans, peas and lentils come in many colors and sizes. The variety is inviting. Dried, they can be stored for months, even years, and still taste delicious when cooked. Legumes contain high quantities of protein and other vital nutrients, but the real bonus is that they taste fantastic and are inexpensive.

We are fortunate in this country to have so many dried legumes available all year long: black turtle, pinto, lima, red and white kidney, chick pea, Navy and Great Northern, Mexican and many others. Dried lentils and dried peas are also plentiful. A mixture of beans is great for casseroles or salads.

Dried lentils and peas take less cooking time than beans. Most dried beans need to be soaked in water overnight. You can, however, eliminate this procedure by the following method: cover beans with water and bring to a boil and continue boiling for about three minutes. Remove pan from heat and let beans soak in this water for 1 hour. Drain and proceed with cooking instructions.

TULLY PLESSER'S "CHULENT" CASSOULET

Tully Plesser, head of a national market and public opinion research firm, shares his family's recipe:

"The fearlessness of Chulent is more in the eating than in the cooking. Chulent is a 'heavy' dish, best served at luncheon when the consumer has ample time for recovery and rehabilitation. Under ideal circumstances, Chulent should not be eaten in quantity unless one has nothing very important to do for several days.

"My father used to say that my mother's Chulent was proof of reincarnation, because if you were able to eat it and wake up the next morning, you were obviously brought back to life. The dish has one socially redeeming feature; it is delicious.

"This family recipe for Chulent has been handed down from generation to generation, together with what has been incorrectly diagnosed as hereditary indigestion. Since weights and measures have never been strong suits in our kitchens, the quantities of ingredients are approximate. Multiply these approximations by one hundred fifty years of cooking Chulent, and you will have some insight into why the results are at times inconsistent.

"Unlike the mysterious formula for Coca-Cola, or the Hostess Secret Chocolate Blend, the recipe has been distributed with an alarming disregard for the well-being of the consumer. There is no doubt in my mind that Chulent should be dispensed by prescription only."

1 large onion, chopped
8 Idaho potatoes, peeled and quartered
1 cup dried lima beans
1 cup dried red kidney beans
½ cup barley
2 pounds flanken or short ribs
1 tablespoon salt
½ teaspoon dry mustard
½ teaspoon dried dill weed
2 bay leaves

Place ingredients in large heavy pot or kettle that can be transferred to the oven. Cover with cold water and bring to a full boil. Cover pot and place in preheated 250 F. oven for 8 hours. Check pot after 5 hours and add a little water, if necessary.

Serves 6 to 8.

SPICY KIDNEY BEANS

2 cups dried kidney beans (1 pound)
2 quarts water
1 tablespoon salt
1 large onion, chopped
2 bay leaves
8 strips bacon
2 tablespoons vegetable oil
4 cloves garlic, minced
1 8-ounce can tomato sauce
1 6-ounce can tomato paste
⅛ teaspoon Tabasco sauce

Soak beans overnight, covered with water. Drain. Add 2 quarts water, salt, onion and bay leaves. Bring to a boil, reduce heat to a simmer and cook for 2 hours, stirring occasionally. A half hour before beans are done, fry bacon in skillet until crisp. Drain on paper towels. Pour off all bacon fat except for 1 tablespoon and add vegetable oil. Saute garlic over low heat for 3 or 4 minutes.

Don't brown. Add remaining ingredients and bacon, stirring until it reaches a boil. Pour sauce into beans and taste for seasoning.

Serve with hot fluffy rice.

Serves 8.

BLACK BEANS

1 pound dried black beans
1½ quarts water
1 quart beef stock
1 clove garlic, minced
1 large onion, chopped
1 green pepper, seeded and chopped
2 stalks celery, chopped
2 bay leaves
½ teaspoon dried oregano
1 teaspoon salt
freshly ground pepper
1 ham hock

Cover beans with water and soak overnight. Drain and place in large heavy pot. Add remaining ingredients. Bring to a boil, reduce heat and simmer for about 2½ hours until tender, stirring occasionally. Discard bay leaves and ham hock. Puree 2 cups of beans in blender or force through food mill. Add to beans in pot and stir.

Serve with hot fluffy rice and fried green plantains.

Serves 8.

NUMPY'S BONAFIDE BOSTON BAKED BEANS

Since he doesn't say much, let alone write things down on paper, few facts are known about Numpy (Norman) Hodgson, a mysterious character who came to Maine from the deep South (Massachusetts) as a young man and settled in Portland. There, he says, he took up minding his own business and going hunting up-country one week every November. To the delight of his cronies, and the cows in the area, he now does more cooking than shooting. Numpy offers two pieces of advice, "short 'n straight," about this old recipe: "Keep the bean pot covered all day and the window open all night."

> 1 pound dry kidney beans
> ⅛ pound salt pork
> 1 ounce brown sugar
> ¼ cup molasses
> 1 medium onion, peeled and quartered
> ½ teaspoon dry mustard
> ⅛ teaspoon pepper
> ½ teaspoon salt

Soak the beans in cold water overnight or for at least 8 hours. Strain, put in a one- or two-quart bean pot, and drop in everything else. Add water until ingredients are just covered. Cover pot. Set oven to bake at 250 F. Go hunting. Remove 8 hours later.

> *Serves (he says) "8 city people of all sexes" or "4 men hunting up-country."*

EASY BAKED BEANS

> 2 tablespoons oil
> 1 medium-large onion, finely chopped
> 1 green pepper, seeded and chopped
> 2 1-pound cans baked beans
> ½ cup brown sugar
> 1 tablespoon Worcestershire sauce
> 8 slices bacon

Heat oil in skillet and saute onion and pepper over medium low heat for 5 minutes. Place onion mixture in bowl and add baked beans, brown sugar and Worcestershire sauce. Combine. Spoon mixture into shallow baking dish and place strips of bacon over top of bean mixture. Bake in preheated 375 F. oven for 20 to 25 minutes until bacon is crisp.

Serves 8.

This dish is perfect to serve with a barbecued meat and a large tossed green salad.

SAM GALLU'S LIMA BEAN STEW

Sam Gallu, a writer and director, gave me this marvelous Roumanian recipe, which provides splendid winter fare.

> 2 cups dried small lima beans
> 2 carrots, peeled and chopped
> 2 medium onions, chopped
> 2 stalks celery with leaves, chopped
> 1 clove garlic, crushed
> 1 bay leaf
> 2 teaspoons salt
> freshly ground pepper to taste
> 1 ham hock
> 3 quarts water
> 2 pounds smoked spareribs
> 2 pounds smoked sausages
> 1 tablespoon Worcestershire sauce

Soak lima beans overnight in water, covered. Drain and place in large heavy pot with carrots, onions, celery, garlic, bay leaf, salt, pepper, ham hock and water. Bring to a boil, reduce heat to a simmer and cook for 1½ hours. Add spareribs which have been cut into 3 or 4 rib pieces and sausages cut into 2-inch lengths. Continue simmering for another hour and a half until meat nearly falls from ribs. Add more water to soup if necessary. During last hour of cooking time add Worcestershire sauce. Check seasoning.

Accompany with black bread, butter and red wine.

Serves 6.

chapter 6. salads

VEGETABLE SALAD

My nephew, Steven, six feet four, age 16, was not at all taken with my gazpacho soup. He watched me chopping vegetables, which he adores, and was shocked when they were "totaled" in the blender. So I composed a salad for him with eight vegetables, partly from his parents' garden, and he approved. I encouraged him to create a dressing and after several bottles of vegetable oil, vinegar, spices, herbs and grimaces, he produced a spectacular Revered Secret Sauce, which you'll find listed under the Salad Dressings.

> 1 head romaine lettuce
> 1 tomato, peeled and cut into wedges
> 4 stalks raw asparagus, cleaned, trimmed and cut into
>   1-inch pieces on a diagonal
> 1 green pepper, seeded and cut into thin strips
> 2 stalks celery, chopped
> 4 radishes, cleaned, trimmed and sliced
> 4 scallions, sliced thin
> ¼ pound mushrooms, cleaned and sliced thin

Place all ingredients in a salad bowl. Prepare ½ cup of Steven Thurston's Revered Secret Sauce and pour over salad. Gently toss.

> *Serves 4 to 6.*

CHICKEN SALAD ABBOTT

> 1 3-pound chicken
> 1 large onion, quartered
> 2 stalks celery, chopped
> 2 carrots, chopped
> 4 sprigs parsley
> ½ teaspoon salt
> ½ cup mayonnaise
> ⅓ cup heavy cream
> juice of ½ lemon
> salt and freshly ground pepper to taste
> 1 cup finely chopped celery
> 1 cup green seedless grapes (optional)

Place chicken, onion, 2 stalks chopped celery, carrots, parsley and salt in large saucepan or pot. Cover with water. Bring to a boil, reduce heat and simmer for 55 minutes. Remove pot from heat and let chicken cool in stock it cooked in. When cool enough to handle, transfer chicken to plate and remove skin and cut meat off bones. Chop meat into bite-size pieces and place in large bowl. Add remaining ingredients and mix well. Spoon onto lettuce leaves or use in sandwich.

Serves 4.

TOMATO SALAD WITH HERB DRESSING

4 lettuce leaves
4 medium ripe tomatoes
2 scallions, finely chopped
1/3 cup olive oil
1 1/2 tablespoons red wine vinegar
1/4 teaspoon dried basil
1/4 teaspoon dried tarragon
1 teaspoon fresh chopped parsley
1/2 teaspoon salt
freshly ground pepper
1/2 teaspoon dry mustard

Place a lettuce leaf on 4 individual salad plates. Cut each tomato in 1/8-inch slices and spread in a row across each leaf. In small bowl mix remaining ingredients with a small wire whisk to make dressing. Check seasoning and spoon equal amounts of dressing over tomatoes.

Serves 4.

TOSSED SALAD

6 romaine lettuce leaves
6 iceberg lettuce leaves
1 small cucumber, peeled and sliced thin
1 ripe tomato, cut into wedges
1/2 green pepper, seeded and chopped
2 scallions, chopped

Tear lettuce leaves into bite-size pieces and place in salad bowl. Add remaining ingredients. Top with favorite dressing and gently toss. Serve immediately.

Serves 4.

ROMAINE LETTUCE AND GRAPEFRUIT SALAD

8 large romaine lettuce leaves
1 cup grapefruit sections
¼ cup sliced toasted almonds

DRESSING:

3 tablespoons vegetable oil
1 tablespoon lemon juice
2 tablespoons grapefruit juice
3 tablespoons heavy cream
½ teaspoon dry mustard
¼ teaspoon sugar
salt and pepper to taste

Break lettuce leaves into bite-size pieces and place in salad bowl. Add grapefruit and almonds. Mix dressing in small bowl with wire whisk and pour over salad. Toss and serve.

Serves 4.

LOBSTER SALAD

Elegant lobster salad is quickly made and a luscious way to treat yourself and your guests.

2 cups chilled cooked lobster meat, coarsely chopped
1 tablespoon grated onion
½ teaspoon dried tarragon
½ teaspoon lemon juice
½ cup mayonnaise (dilute with 2 tablespoons heavy cream, if desired)
salt and freshly ground pepper to taste

Combine lobster with remaining ingredients and serve on crisp
lettuce leaves with slices of ripe tomato and freshly made toast
with sweet butter. And champagne, of course.

Serves 4.

SALAD NIÇOISE

I first had Salad Niçoise in the South of France and it's been a favorite summer salad since then. The combination of ingredients
produces a unique flavor and it is a salad of substance.

> *1 medium head romaine lettuce*
> *4 boiled potatoes, peeled and sliced*
> *8 black olives*
> *1 7-ounce can white meat tuna*
> *2 tomatoes, cut into wedges*
> *1 cup cooked green beans*
> *1 green pepper, seeded and sliced into strips*
> *1 tablespoon capers*
> *4 anchovies, chopped*
> *½ cup Vinaigrette Dressing (See index for recipe)*

Tear lettuce into bite-size pieces. Arrange across bottom of salad
bowl. Place potatoes, olives, tuna, tomatoes, green beans, green
pepper, capers and anchovies over lettuce. Pour dressing over
salad and gently toss.
Serve with crusty bread and red or white wine.

Serves 4.

KIDNEY BEAN SALAD WITH TUNA

1 pound canned red kidney beans, drained
1 7-ounce can white meat tuna, drained and flaked
2 hard-boiled eggs, chopped
¼ cup sweet pickles, chopped
1 small onion, minced
¼ teaspoon salt
freshly ground pepper to taste
½ cup mayonnaise

Combine ingredients and chill thoroughly.

Serves 4 to 6.

GREEK SALAD

6 leaves romaine lettuce
1 small head iceberg lettuce
8 black olives (Greek, if possible)
1 small cucumber, peeled and diced
2 ripe tomatoes, diced
½ pound feta cheese, crumbled
1 small red onion, peeled and cut in rings
capers or anchovies to taste

DRESSING:

3 tablespoons lemon
½ cup olive oil
2 tablespoons dried oregano
½ teaspoon salt
freshly ground pepper to taste

Tear lettuce into bite-size pieces and put in salad bowl. Add remaining ingredients. Combine salad dressing and pour over salad. Toss.

Serves 4 to 6.

SHRIMP SALAD

A pure shrimp salad that isn't filled with celery is a glorious thing indeed. It makes a fine sandwich filling or is good eaten plain.

1 pound cooked shrimp, shelled and deveined
1 scallion, minced
1 teaspoon fresh chopped parsley
1 teaspoon fresh chopped dill
1 teaspoon lemon juice
⅓ cup mayonnaise or as needed

Combine ingredients, cover and refrigerate several hours before serving.

Serves 3 to 4.

WALDORF SALAD

Waldorf Salad must be a masculine favorite, judging from the number of men who want to know how to make this crunchy salad.

2 large Delicious apples, cored and diced
2 stalks celery, finely chopped
1 cup seedless green grapes
⅔ cup walnut pieces
½ cup mayonnaise
1 teaspoon lemon juice
dash of salt
½ teaspoon sugar

Place apples, celery, grapes and walnuts in bowl. Mix together remaining ingredients and pour over salad. Gently toss and serve immediately or chill for several hours before serving.

Serves 4.

FRESH SPINACH SALAD WITH BACON

1 pound fresh spinach, washed, dried, stemmed and
    broken into bite-size pieces
½ cup crumbled cooked bacon
1 cup finely sliced raw mushrooms
1 small red onion, thinly sliced
½ cup Vinaigrette Dressing (See index for recipe.)

Place spinach in salad bowl. Top with bacon, mushrooms and
onions. Pour dressing over salad and toss.

Serves 4 to 6.

ROAST BEEF SALAD

1 medium head romaine lettuce
¾ pound sliced roast beef, cut into thin strips
1 cup diced cooked boiling potatoes
2 hard-boiled eggs, coarsely chopped
1 small red onion, coarsely chopped
1 tablespoon fresh chopped parsley
1 heaping tablespoon capers
⅔ cup Vinaigrette Dressing

Arrange broken pieces of romaine lettuce in salad bowl. Next
place roast beef, potatoes and eggs over lettuce. Sprinkle with
onion, parsley and capers. Pour dressing over top and gently toss.
    Serve with crusty French bread and sweet butter and white
wine.

Serves 4.

GREEN GODDESS SALAD DRESSING

I first tasted Green Goddess Dressing at the London Chop House
in Detroit. It was the most interesting "creamy" salad dressing I'd
ever had. Unable to get their exact recipe "because it is made in
large quantities," I greedily tested and researched mixtures until I
found this comparable dressing.

1 cup mayonnaise
1 tablespoon anchovy paste
1 clove garlic, crushed
2 ½ tablespoons tarragon vinegar, or 2 ½ tablespoons
       wine vinegar and ½ teaspoon dried tarragon
1 scallion, finely chopped
2 teaspoons finely chopped parsley

Combine ingredients, cover and chill for several hours. Serve on mixed lettuce salad with cucumbers.

Makes about 1 ¼ cups.

RUSSIAN DRESSING

1 cup mayonnaise
¼ cup ketchup
2 tablespoons minced pickle
2 tablespoons minced green pepper
1 tablespoon minced onion or scallion
1 teaspoon lemon juice
freshly ground pepper

Combine ingredients well and chill thoroughly.

Makes about 1 ½ cups.

STEVEN THURSTON'S SECRET SALAD SAUCE

¾ cup vegetable oil
¼ cup wine vinegar or to taste
1 heaping teaspoon prepared mustard
1 teaspoon salt
½ teaspoon dried basil
¼ teaspoon dried tarragon
1 clove crushed garlic
plenty of freshly ground pepper

Place ingredients in bowl and beat with wire whisk until thickened.

>*Makes 1 cup. To make ½ cup just reduce recipe by half.*

VINAIGRETTE SAUCE

½ cup olive or vegetable oil
3 tablespoons red wine vinegar
½ teaspoon dry mustard
½ teaspoon salt
freshly ground pepper

Place ingredients in small bowl and mix vigorously with wire whisk.

>*Yield: about ⅔ cup.*

For vinaigrette variations, mix one of the following with the above recipe:

Anchovy: 3 anchovy filets, crushed with 1 tablespoon minced scallions.

Garlic: 2 crushed cloves garlic.

Herb: ¼ teaspoon dried tarragon, ¼ teaspoon dried chives and ¼ teaspoon dill.

Italian: 1 crushed clove of garlic, ¼ teaspoon dried oregano and ¼ teaspoon seasoned salt.

Lemon: Use 3 tablespoons fresh lemon juice in place of red wine vinegar.

Mustard: 1 teaspoon prepared mustard instead of dry mustard.

Onion: 1 tablespoon minced onion.

Roquefort: 2 tablespoons crumbled Roquefort cheese and 2 tablespoons of heavy cream.

Chapter 7. main courses

chicken
turkey
beef
lamb
pork
veal
fish
shellfish

CHICKEN AND TURKEY

Poultry is versatile, plentiful and still relatively cheap. Since it can be sauteed, fried, braised, poached, baked, roasted, stewed, and grilled, and used for any course except dessert, chicken several times a week need not seem repetitious. The dish in which it is used can be simple or elaborate, and an entirely different taste can be elicited by the use of spices and sauces. In fact, many cooks have started substituting chicken breasts for veal in such dishes as Veal Cordon Bleu. One friend, a roast chicken addict, invents a new stuffing or sauce for his favorite dish each time he serves it.

Look for smooth moist skin (not torn or bruised), a full breast and a flexible breastbone, when you are buying chicken or other birds. If you are lucky enough to be near a store that sells fresh chicken, always buy your poultry there. If you haven't had fresh-killed chicken lately, you will be amazed at the difference in taste.

Chicken is perishable and should be cooked the day it is purchased, or frozen until ready to use. To thaw a chicken leave it in the refrigerator overnight or place it, completely wrapped, under cold water in the sink for a few hours. It should be cooked immediately after thawing.

Capon and turkey will take longer to thaw since they are larger birds. Allow an extra half day to a day for them if thawing in the refrigerator, or a few more hours under cold water, if that method is used. Always keep the bird in its wrapper when thawing so the taste won't be affected.

Chickens are classified according to age and size for different cooking methods:

	WEIGHT	COOKING METHODS
Broiler (10 to 14 weeks old)	1½ to 2½ lbs.	broil or grill
Fryer (14 to 20 weeks old)	2½ to 3½ lbs.	fry, saute, roast, boil, poach, fricasse or for casserole
Capon (7 to 10 months old)	5 to 8 lbs.	roast, fricassee or for casserole
Fowl (11 months or older)	4 to 6 lbs.	stew or fricassee

BILL ALLER'S CHICKEN
AND RICE CASSEROLE

Bill Aller is the New York Times *food photographer. He's taken food photos for* House and Garden *and* Holiday *magazines and has photographed food layouts for several cookbooks. He's traveled around the world shooting pictures of food and says a soufflé is the most difficult dish to photograph. He comes from Ohio, and recalls that children in his family were not allowed into the real dining room until they were able to eat with proper manners and not talk at the table.*

His first experience as a cook came when he worked for his Boy Scout Cooking Merit Badge. He was very anxious about the test: to bake a potato. He shopped for the perfect potato, which turned out to be perfect, but enormous. When all the other scouts' potatoes were done, his beauty was rock hard in the middle. His understanding scout master awarded him his cooking badge anyway, noting that longer cooking would have produced a fine baked potato and hoping that a valuable lesson had been learned.

The dish that follows is one he improvised successfully several years ago.

> ¾ cup rice
> 1 can cream of celery soup
> 1 can cream of mushroom soup
> 1 can water
> 1 tablespoon chopped parsley
> 6 to 8 pieces chicken
> 1 envelope onion soup mix

Combine rice, celery and mushroom soups, water and parsley. Place in baking dish. Place chicken pieces across top and sprinkle with onion soup mix. Cover with foil and bake in 350 F. oven for about 2 hours. Don't lift foil until cooking time is over.

Serves 4.

ARROZ CON POLLO

8 serving pieces chicken
salt and pepper
3 tablespoons olive oil
2 medium onions, chopped
2 cloves garlic, crushed
1 green pepper, seeded and chopped
1 8-ounce can whole tomatoes, chopped
½ teaspoon salt
¼ teaspoon saffron
1 teaspoon paprika
¼ teaspoon dried oregano
2½ cups chicken broth
1 bay leaf, crumbled
1¼ cup long grain rice
1 cup green peas
1 2-ounce jar pimento strips

Pat chicken dry and season with salt and pepper. Heat oil in skillet and brown chicken on both sides. Transfer to 4-quart casserole. Saute onions, garlic and green pepper for 5 minutes. Add tomatoes, salt, saffron, paprika, oregano, chicken broth and bay leaf. Bring to a boil. Sprinkle rice over chicken and pour onion mixture over top. Add green peas, stir, cover and bake in preheated 350 F. oven for 45 minutes until chicken is tender and rice cooked.
   Garnish with pimento strips.

Serves 4.

BASQUE-STYLE CHICKEN

8 serving pieces chicken
3 tablespoons olive oil
1 medium-large onion, sliced
2 green peppers, seeded and chopped
1 8-ounce can tomatoes, chopped
¼ cup chicken stock
½ cup dry white wine
salt and freshly ground pepper
1 tablespoon freshly chopped parsley

Wash chicken and pat dry with paper towels. Heat oil in skillet and brown chicken on both sides. Remove chicken and set aside. Add onion and peppers and cook for 5 minutes over medium low heat. Add chicken, tomatoes, stock and wine. Bring to a boil, reduce heat and simmer for 10 minutes. Turn each piece of chicken and cook for 12 minutes more. Check seasoning and use a little salt and pepper. Transfer to serving dish and sprinkle with parsley.

Serve with hot fluffy rice.

> Serves 4.

THE BEST FRIED CHICKEN

This is my grandmother Eva Lowe's recipe for The Best Fried Chicken I've ever eaten. The recipe is simple: the secret is having a freshly killed chicken. I remember her picking out a hen, wringing its neck and plucking the feathers. Soon the aroma of the fresh chicken cooking in the kitchen made it impossible to think of anything but "When will it be ready?" Accompanying the chicken would be corn on the cob, fried okra, a sliced tomato salad and corn bread. We had chicken several times a week because my grandfather preferred it over all other meat.

> 8 serving pieces of fresh-killed chicken
> salt and pepper
> 1 cup flour
> 1 cup vegetable oil or lard

Wash the chicken pieces under water, shaking off extra water. Season well with salt and pepper. Dredge chicken pieces in flour. Heat oil in skillet and add chicken. Cook over medium-high heat for 10 minutes. Turn each piece. Lower heat to medium and cook chicken for 10 minutes, then turn again. Cook 10 more minutes.

> Serves 4.

ROBERT BUNIM'S CHICKEN OREGANO

Successful cooks always have their special secrets. Bobby Bunim, an executive at CBS, claims the secret of his cooking success is sipping scotch. The great chef Fernand Point felt sure that after even one cocktail the palate was unable to distinguish what was great and what was merely adequate. But I've tasted Bobby's chicken and it's great. So, his palate must be the exception. This recipe actually originated with Bobby's friend Lou Scanna's eighty-five-year-old Italian mother. He has added his own improvements, of course.

> 8 serving pieces chicken
> salt and freshly ground pepper to taste
> 3 tablespoons butter
> 2 cloves garlic, cut into slivers
> ½ teaspoon dried oregano
> 1 large onion, sliced
> juice of 2 lemons

Grease a 14-inch oval or rectangular-shaped shallow baking dish. Place chicken in dish skin-side-down and season with salt and pepper. Turn chicken and salt and pepper again. Place piece of butter and garlic on each piece of chicken, sprinkle with oregano and arrange onion rings across chicken. Cover dish with aluminum foil and bake in preheated 325 F. oven for 15 minutes. Remove foil and pour lemon juice over chicken. Re-cover with foil and bake for 30 more minutes. Turn heat to 350, remove foil and cook for about 30 minutes, basting with juices in pan. As onions turn golden, they can be pushed into sauce and when chicken has browned nicely, dish is done.

> *Serves 4.*

CHICKEN BAKED IN ORANGE SAUCE

8 serving pieces chicken
¼ teaspoon salt
freshly ground pepper
2 tablespoons butter
1 tablespoon vegetable oil
¾ cup orange juice
1 tablespoon grated orange rind
1 teaspoon paprika
½ teaspoon dry mustard
pinch of ginger, freshly grated
2 tablespoons melted butter

Season chicken with salt and pepper. Heat butter and oil in sauce-pan. Brown chicken on each side. Place in baking dish 1½ inches deep. Combine remaining ingredients. Pour over chicken and bake in preheated 375 F. oven for about 1 hour. Turn chicken after 30 minutes.

Serves 4.

CHICKEN-FILLED TACOS

2 chicken breasts, boned and skinned
salt and pepper
2 tablespoons vegetable oil
1 green pepper, cored, seeded and chopped fine
2 scallions, chopped fine
8 tacos (El Paso packaged brand is good)
1 cup shredded iceberg lettuce
¾ cup shredded cheddar cheese
1 8-ounce can taco sauce

Cut chicken breasts into small bite-size pieces. Season with salt and pepper. Heat oil in skillet and add chicken pieces. Turn chicken with spatula until pieces are cooked and turn white with a little gold color. Remove and drain on paper towels. Place chicken in bowl with green pepper and scallions. Fill tacos with equal amounts of chicken mixture. Sprinkle equal amounts of shredded lettuce, cheese and taco sauce over tacos. Place in preheated 400 F. oven on cookie sheet and bake until cheese melts.

Serves 4.

CHICKEN NORMANDY

When my friend, student John Gitlin, is preparing a "real meal," he calls me from Harvard for my recipe for Chicken Normandy. Each time I give him the recipe he says, "It needs more garlic." For those who cherish the potent clove, add one or two more.

>   8 serving pieces chicken
>   salt and freshly ground pepper
>   2 tablespoons butter
>   1 tablespoon vegetable oil
>   1 medium onion, chopped
>   1 clove garlic, crushed
>   1 cup apple juice
>   ½ pound fresh mushrooms, sliced
>   2 cooking apples, peeled, cored and sliced
>   ¼ cup Calvados or brandy
>   1 tablespoon flour

Wash chicken pieces and pat dry. Season well with salt and pepper. Heat butter and oil in large skillet and brown chicken on both sides. Add onion and garlic, then turn each piece of chicken. Pour apple juice over chicken, bring to a boil, reduce heat, cover and simmer for 10 minutes. Add mushrooms, apples and Calvados or brandy. Re-cover and simmer for 15 minutes. Transfer chicken to heated serving dish with tongs. With a large slotted spoon remove onions, mushrooms and apples and spoon over top of chicken. Mix flour with 2 tablespoons water and stir to make a smooth paste. Add several tablespoons of hot sauce to mixture in pan and stir. Stir over high heat until sauce has thickened slightly. Check seasoning and pour over chicken. Garnish with fresh chopped parsley.

Serves 4.

CHICKEN SAUTE WITH HERBS

8 serving pieces of chicken
salt and pepper
flour
2 tablespoons butter
1 tablespoon vegetable oil
1 medium onion, chopped
½ teaspoon dried thyme
1 tablespoon fresh chopped parsley
1 tablespoon lemon juice
¼ cup chicken broth

Pat chicken pieces dry. Season with salt and pepper. Dredge with flour. Heat butter and oil in skillet. Brown on each side. Add onion, sprinkle with remaining ingredients. Turn chicken pieces, cover and simmer for 15 minutes. Turn chicken, re-cover and simmer for 10 to 15 minutes until chicken is tender.

Serves 4.

CHICKEN TANDOORI

A single long-stemmed red rose was delivered to my apartment the day after I served Chicken Tandoori to a New York politician. The note read, "I've been looking for this Chicken Tandoori all my life. Please send recipe."

1 3½-pound chicken, quartered (backbone removed)
1 cup plain yoghurt
3 cloves garlic, crushed
1 teaspoon cinnamon
1 teaspoon cumin
1 teaspoon turmeric
1 teaspoon ginger
2 teaspoons coriander
pinch of cayenne pepper
salt and freshly ground pepper to taste
3 tablespoons fresh lime juice
3 tablespoons melted butter

2 cups vegetable oil
3 medium onions, sliced thin
4 slices fresh lime

Combine ingredients yoghurt through lime juice in large bowl. Prick chicken quarters in several pieces and place in bowl with mixture. Turn pieces until well coated, cover and refrigerate overnight. Place chicken pieces in greased shallow baking dish skin-side-up. Sprinkle each quarter with a little melted butter and cook in preheated 350 F. oven for 45 to 50 minutes, basting with butter occasionally. Meanwhile, heat oil in deep saucepan. Deep-fry onion rings until golden brown. Drain. When chicken is cooked, garnish each quarter with equal amounts of onion rings and a slice of lime.

Serves 4.

MARINATED FRIED CHICKEN

8 serving pieces chicken
½ cup olive oil
2 cloves garlic, crushed
2 tablespoons lemon juice
½ teaspoon dried oregano
½ teaspoon dried basil
salt and freshly ground pepper to taste
flour
½ cup vegetable oil

Wash chicken and pat dry. Combine olive oil, garlic, lemon juice, oregano, basil and salt and pepper in bowl. Add chicken and turn until well coated with marinade. Cover and refrigerate for several hours. Dredge chicken pieces in flour. Heat oil and fry chicken until golden brown about 12 minutes each side.

Serves 4.

OVEN-BARBECUED CHICKEN

8 serving pieces chicken
1 8-ounce can tomato sauce
1 clove garlic, crushed
1 teaspoon prepared mustard
¼ cup vinegar
1 tablespoon Worcestershire sauce
1 teaspoon sugar
¼ teaspoon salt
2 tablespoons oil
3 onions, thinly sliced

Place chicken pieces in shallow baking dish. Combine all ingredients, except for chicken, in saucepan. Bring to a boil, reduce heat and simmer for 15 minutes. Pour sauce over chicken pieces. Bake in preheated 400 F. oven for 30 minutes. Reduce heat to 350 F. and cook for 30 minutes longer.

Serves 4.

PETTI DI POLLO ALLA BOLOGNESE

2 large chicken breasts, skinned, boned and cut in half
salt and freshly ground pepper to taste
flour
2 tablespoons butter
1 tablespoon vegetable oil
¼ pound thinly sliced prosciutto
8 ounces bel paese cheese
2 tablespoons grated Parmesan cheese
½ cup chicken stock
¼ cup dry sherry

Place each chicken breast half between 2 sheets of waxed paper and flatten slightly with flat side of tenderizer or rolling pin. Trim breasts so that they are all the same size. Season chicken with salt and pepper. Dust with flour. Heat butter and oil in large skillet and quickly brown each side of chicken over medium high heat. Lay breasts in buttered shallow baking dish. Top each breast half with slices of prosciutto and a slice of bel paese. Sprinkle with Parmesan cheese. Pour chicken stock and sherry into dish and place in preheated 350 F. oven for 10 minutes. Place under broiler for two minutes until lightly browned on top.

Serves 4.

ROAST CHICKEN À LA BOUQUETIÈRE

A *bouquetière* is an assortment of cooked fresh vegetables, often arranged in the shape of a bouquet, which serves as a garnish for meat dishes. It is a very attractive and delicious way to serve seasonal vegetables. Each vegetable is cooked individually, retaining its own distinct flavor. The vegetables are grouped around a roast meat, in this case, chicken, and then are topped with Hollandaise Sauce. Roast Chicken à la Bouquetière is a feast fit for a king.

ROAST CHICKEN:

> 1 4-pound roasting chicken
> salt and freshly ground pepper
> 2 tablespoons melted butter for basting

Wash chicken and pat dry with paper towels or clean dish towel. Season chicken cavity with salt and pepper. Truss bird in the following manner: With a piece of white kitchen string a little over a yard long, wind the center of the string around drumstick ends and tie together crossing the drumsticks. Push the drumsticks and legs up against the breast. Pull the string ends between the legs and sides of the breast. Turn chicken over and bring string through and around the center joint of each wing, and tie together. Fold each wing tip back. Brush melted butter over breast and legs of chicken in roasting pan and put in preheated 350 F. oven. Roast for about 1 hour and 15 minutes, basting occasionally with butter. Test for doneness by piercing the flesh of the thickest part of the lower thigh. If the juice that is expelled runs clear, the chicken is done. If juice is pink, it requires further cooking.

When chicken has roasted 45 minutes or so, prepare vegetables:

BOUQUETIÈRE:

1½ pounds new potatoes
1 small head cauliflower, broken into small flowerets
¾ pound fresh string beans, ends trimmed and left
    whole
1 pound carrots, peeled and cut into 1-inch lengths

In saucepan, bring enough water to cover potatoes to a boil. Add potatoes and cook for about 18 minutes until tender. In each of three different saucepans place 1 cup of water and ½ cup of chicken broth and bring to a boil. Add a vegetable to each pan, cover and simmer until vegetables are tender, approximately 10 minutes. Drain each vegetable as cooked and place in large bake-proof dish in groups. Dot with butter, cover with foil and keep warm. When chicken is done, remove trussing string and place in center of heated serving platter. Arrange vegetables around chicken and return platter to oven, and prepare Hollandaise Sauce.

BLENDER HOLLANDAISE SAUCE:

3 egg yolks
1½ tablespoons lemon juice
¼ teaspoon salt
pinch cayenne pepper
1 stick sweet butter (4 ounces)

Place egg yolks, lemon juice, salt and cayenne pepper in blender. Melt butter in saucepan over medium low heat. Cover blender jar and turn on low speed. Remove center of lid and slowly pour in hot butter.

Spoon Hollandaise over vegetables and garnish with fresh chopped parsley.

Serves 4.

ROAST TURKEY

1 12-pound turkey, fresh or thawed
salt and pepper
butter

Remove giblets from turkey and save to prepare stock. (Instructions below.) Season cavity of turkey with salt and pepper. Pat turkey dry. Put large sheet of wide heavy-duty foil across roasting pan. Place turkey in center. Baste with butter. Cover wing tips with small pieces of foil. Bring foil up around bird. It doesn't need to be sealed air-tight. Use two sheets of foil if you're roasting a large bird. Roast in preheated 450 F. oven for about 3 hours and 10 minutes (about 18 to 20 minutes per pound). Turn the foil back during last 30 minutes of cooking time so turkey can brown. Baste with butter.

Makes about 2 cups.

GIBLET GRAVY:

turkey giblets *
1 medium onion, quartered
2 stalks celery and leaves, chopped
2 carrots, chopped
2 sprigs parsley
½ teaspoon dried thyme
2 crumbled bay leaves
1 teaspoon salt
2 quarts water
freshly ground pepper to taste
2 tablespoons flour

Place all ingredients except flour in large saucepan. Bring to a boil and simmer for 2 hours. Strain. When turkey has cooked, take several tablespoons of juice from bottom of pan and add to turkey stock. Heat stock. In small bowl mix flour with 3 tablespoons water until smooth. Add several tablespoons hot turkey stock to this mixture and mix, then pour into boiling stock. Stir until sauce

---

*Giblets are the heart, gizzard and liver of a fowl. They are usually wrapped and, with the neck, placed inside the bird by the butcher. Use the neck, heart and gizzard to make gravy but not the liver, which disintegrates in stock. If you want, saute the liver in butter, and chop it to add to the gravy at the last minute. Or freeze the livers and when you have a good collection make a pâté or saute them with sherry and butter.

has thickened. Check seasoning. Serve with turkey in heated sauceboat.

BASIC TURKEY STUFFING

1 stick butter
1 clove garlic, crushed
1 cup chopped onion
3 stalks celery, chopped
2 8-ounce packages herb seasoned stuffing
2 eggs, lightly beaten
1/2 teaspoon sage
3/4 cup chicken broth
1/4 cup fresh chopped parsley

Melt 3 tablespoons butter in skillet and saute garlic, onion and celery for 5 minutes. Place stuffing mix in large bowl. Add onion mixture. Melt remaining butter and add to mixture in bowl with remaining ingredients. Mix thoroughly. Stuffing mixture should be thoroughly moistened, but not wet or stuffing will be soggy.

Stuff turkey but don't pack tightly, because it will expand during cooking. Truss cavity closed and tie legs together. Spoon stuffing into neck cavity and secure skin to back of bird with small metal skewer.

Stuffing for 12- to 14-pound turkey.

Bake extra stuffing in well-greased baking pan until golden on top about 35 minutes.

Stuffed turkey will require extra cooking time. Allow about 2 minutes extra time per pound of bird. A 14-pound turkey stuffed will need about 25 minutes more cooking.

Stuffing is an area where your creativity can really come to the fore. Mix in a pound of sausage and use only one package of prepared stuffing. Add sauteed almonds intead of celery. Or invent your own variation.

BEEF, LAMB, PORK AND VEAL

Knowing how to select the right cut of meat for a dish is equally as important as cooking it properly. For the uninitiated, the most direct route to learning cuts and quality of meat is to befriend a good butcher. He represents, sadly, a dwindling profession. More and more we must shop in supermarkets that present us with a bewildering array of neatly packaged meats to select from. Without wasting money or a good piece of meat, the question remains of how to determine quality and the cut of meat necessary. Some of this work has been done by our government. Federal inspection of meat by the USDA insures that the meat in our markets are not diseased; the quality is measured in 5 grades. The USDA seals of inspection and grading are stamped on the meat with a harmless vegetable dye. By the time it is cut, packaged and placed in the refrigerator case ready for purchase, we seldom see the once-familiar purple lettering, but rest assured that the store buyer has done his checking.

The grading for meat is based on the conformation of the animal, the quality or tenderness and palatability of the flesh, and the amount of usable meat on the carcass now designated by yield numbering.

The following chart will show you how meats are graded:

BEEF	VEAL	LAMB	PORK
Prime	Prime	Prime	U.S. No. 1
Choice	Choice	Choice	U.S. No. 2
Good	Good	Good	U.S. No. 3
Standard	Standard	Utility	U.S. No. 4
Commercial	Utility	Cull	Utility

Retail markets rarely will sell any meat graded below Good (U.S. No. 3).

After finding a market we can trust, one that regularly provides good fresh meat, we begin to learn how to go about selecting it. The label on each package of meat should give the grading, cut of the meat, price per pound and actual cost—all factors to consider when buying the meat.

Before going into selection of the cut of meat, which follows in detail, here are some pointers on inspecting the meat you are about to purchase.

COLOR

Beef and lamb should be bright pink/red, but not dark in color. Veal and pork should be light pink or whitish in color with no darkened edges. The fat should be whiter than the meat.

FAT

Excess fat is unacceptable, because you're paying for it at the same price as the meat and it will have to be trimmed off. The color of fat should be creamy white, never yellow.

MARBLING

Marbling or interior fat, in beef, resembles tiny white dots in the most tender meat and thin strokes of white in stewing meat such as chuck. Heavy marbling indicates the meat will be old, fat and tough, so pass it by.

MEAT CUT SELECTION

The inexperienced when uncertain tend to buy a more expensive cut of meat, thinking it's bound to turn out successfully; but using costly sirloin in Grandpa's Irish Stew is money lost. Less expensive chuck, cubed and cooked properly, is the right choice for any tender juicy beef stew.

The following list contains the most common cuts of meat, and cooking methods for beef, lamb, pork and veal. This list should start you off to a good beginning into the challenging business of meat-cut selection.

NOTE: The quality or more tender cuts of meat respond well to cooking by dry heat: roasting, broiling or sauteeing. Less tender cuts require slower cooking with moisture: braising or stewing.

BEEF

CUT	COOKING METHOD
BRISKET	
Front cut	Braise or Stew
Flat half	Braise or Stew
Edge cut	Braise or Stew
CHUCK	
Arm Pot Roast	Braise
Blade Pot Roast	Braise
Boneless Shoulder Pot Roast	Braise
Boston or English Roast	Braise
Chicken Steaks	Braise or Saute if tenderized
Short Ribs	Braise
(Any section ground)	Broil or Saute
FLANK	
Flank Steak	Broil or Roast
(Excellent used in sliced Chinese dishes)	Stir-fry
ROUND	
Bottom Round (Pot Roast)	Braise
Cube Steak	Saute if tenderized
Eye of Round Roast	Braise
Rump	Braise or Roast if high in quality
Round Steak	Braise
SIRLOIN	
Tip Roast	Roast
Steaks	Broil or Saute
SHORT LOIN	
Tenderloin (whole)	Saute and Roast
Cut into tournedoes or filet mignon	Saute or Roast
Steaks (T-Bone, Porterhouse, Club, Shell— also called New York or Kansas City Strips) or Delmonico	Broil or Saute

RIB

Standing Rib Roast	Roast
Rib Steak	Broil or Saute
Delmonico Roast (boned)	Roast

PLATE

Ribs and Spareribs	Roast or Braise

LAMB

CUT	COOKING METHOD
LEG	
Whole	Roast
Boned and Butterflied	Barbecue
Center Cut	Roast or Braise
Frenched	Roast
Leg Steaks	Broil or Saute
Cubed for Kebabs	Broil or Saute
LOIN	
Saddle	Roast
Chops	Broil
Rack	Roast
Crown Rack (two racks)	Roast
SHOULDER	
Steaks	Braise or Stew
BREAST	
Rolled or Stuffed	Braise, Roast or Broil

(Any section of lamb may be used for ground lamb or stewing.)

PORK

CUT	COOKING METHOD
LEG (Ham—Fresh or Smoked)	
Whole Ham	Roast or Braise
Butt Half	Roast or Braise
Center Roast	Roast or Braise
Boned and Rolled Center	Roast or Braise
Shank Roast Portion	Roast or Braise
Sliced Ham Steak	Broil or Saute
LOIN	
Sirloin Roast	Roast
Boned and Rolled Roast	Roast or Braise
Sirloin Chops	Broil, Saute or Roast
Center Loin Roast	Roast or Braise
Blade Loin Roast	Roast or Braise
Tenderloin	Saute and Roast
Top Loin Chops	Broil, Saute or Roast
Back Ribs (Country Style)	Roast, Braise or Barbecue
Spareribs	Roast, Braise or Barbecue
SHOULDER	
Boston Butt, Shoulder Roast or Pork Butt	Roast or Braise
Picnic Shoulder	Roast or Braise

VEUAL

CUT	COOKING METHOD
BREAST	
Whole	Braise
Ribs	Braise
Boned and Stuffed Breast	Roast or Braise
SHANK	
Steaks	Braise
SHOULDER	
Arm Roast	Braise or Roast
Arm Steaks	Braise or Saute
Blade Roast	Braise or Roast
Blade Steaks	Braise or Saute
Neck	Braise or Stew
RIB ROAST	
Rack	Roast
Rib Chops	Broil or Saute
LOIN	
Roast	Roast
Boned and Rolled Roast	Roast or Braise
Chops	Broil or Saute
Kidney Chops	Broil or Saute
LEG	
Sirloin Roast	Roast
Rump Roast	Roast
Tip Roast	Roast
Center Leg	Roast
Shank (for Osso Buco)	Braise
Cutlets (flattened for Scaloppini)	Saute

(Any section may be used ground for patties or stuffings or cubed for stew.)

VARIETY MEATS

Brains: Beef, lamb, pork or veal—poach or saute
Chitterlings: Small intestines of calf—saute or fry
Feet: Pig, lamb or calf—braise or pickle
Head: lamb or veal—braise
Heart: Beef, lamb, pork or veal—saute
Kidney: Lamb, pork or veal—saute or braise
Liver: Lamb, pork or veal—saute or broil
Sweet Breads: From pancreas and throat of
    lamb and veal—braise or saute
Tongue: Beef, lamb, pork or veal (fresh or
    smoked)—boil
Tripe: Stomach of beef—braise or stew

FROZEN MEATS

Frozen meat should be thoroughly defrosted before cooking it. For best results, allow meat to thaw in original wrapping in refrigerator overnight. If time doesn't permit this, thaw at room temperature in original wrapping in a plate or dish, and cook immediately. If you are not going to cook thawed meat for half an hour or more, refrigerate it in wrapping until ready to use.

STANDING RIB ROAST

6- to 8-pound rib roast
½ teaspoon dried thyme
½ teaspoon rosemary
salt and pepper

Rub herbs, salt and pepper into roast. Insert meat thermometer into thickest part of meat (not touching bone or fat). Place roast on rack on shallow roasting pan, bone-side-down. Cook until the thermometer reads 140 F. for medium-rate, about 20 minutes per pound. Allow roast to rest 20 minutes before carving.

ALL-DAY METHOD:

Place roast in preheated 400 F. oven prepared as described above at noon. Cook for 1 hour and turn off oven. Don't open door of oven and leave roast in oven until 7 p.m. Turn oven on to 400 F. and cook for about 35 minutes. Remove to platter and let rest for 20 minutes before carving.

Serves 6 to 8.

ROAST BEEF GRAVY:

3 tablespoons fat from roasting pan
2 tablespoons flour
2 cups beef stock, heated
¼ teaspoon dried thyme
salt and pepper to taste

Place fat in saucepan. Stir in flour. Add hot stock slowly, constantly stirring. Sprinkle with seasoning and serve in sauce boat with roast.

Yield: About 2 cups.

INDIVIDUAL BEEF PIES

2 tablespoons olive oil
1 medium onion, finely chopped
2 cloves garlic, crushed
½ green pepper, finely chopped
1 pound ground chuck
16 pitted black olives, chopped
⅓ cup raisins
1 tablespoon vinegar
1 tablespoon paprika
1 teaspoon dried oregano
½ cup tomato paste
½ teaspoon salt
freshly ground pepper to taste
double amount of pie crust recipe (See index for recipe.)

Heat oil and saute onion, garlic, green pepper and ground beef, stirring often, until beef loses pink color. Add olives, raisins, vinegar, paprika, oregano, tomato paste, salt and pepper. Combine well and simmer for about 5 minutes. Remove mixture from heat and allow it to cool. Roll dough out onto sheet about ⅛-inch thick. Cut into as many 3½- or 4-inch circles as you can (approximately 10). Place a heaping tablespoon of mixture in center. Bring one edge of circle over to meet other edge and secure by pressing semi-circle with tines of fork. Prick top of each pie with fork to allow air to escape. Place on greased baking sheet in preheated 400 F. oven and cook until crust is golden, about 10 to 12 minutes.

Serves 4.

DEVILED BEEF BONES

This recipe is a standard but was inspired by my brother Jody, who wanted me to "do something good with the leftover bones."

> 6 rib bones from cooked rib roast, cut into individual
>   bones
> 1 cup bread crumbs
> 1 teaspoon dry mustard
> ¼ teaspoon Tabasco
> ¼ teaspoon dried oregano
> salt and pepper to taste
> ⅔ cup melted butter

Combine bread crumbs, mustard, Tabasco, oregano and salt and pepper. Brush bones with butter and roll in crumb mixture. Broil several inches from heat until browned on all sides, being very careful not to disturb crumbs when turning them. Serve with sauce on the side.

DEVILED BEEF BONE SAUCE:

> 2 tablespoons A-1 sauce
> ½ cup ketchup
> ½ teaspoon sugar
> 1 teaspoon prepared mustard
> 2 tablespoons mayonnaise
> 1 tablespoon grated onion.

Combine ingredients and serve.

Serves 2.

LONDON BROIL

2- to 2½-pound flank steak
1 large clove garlic, cut in half
1 tablespoon soy sauce
2 tablespoons vegetable oil
salt and pepper to taste

Remove extra fat from steak. Rub steak with garlic halves on each side. Combine soy sauce and oil and brush both sides of steak. Season with salt and pepper. Place on broiling rack under broiler about 2 inches from heat. Cook for 6 minutes. Turn and cook 6 minutes on second side or until desired doneness. Cut into thin slices on a diagonal.

Serves 4 to 6.

MARINATED FLANK STEAK

2½- to 3-pound flank steak

MARINADE:

1 large clove garlic, crushed
¼ cup soy sauce
1 cup barbecue sauce
¼ teaspoon dried oregano
½ teaspoon salt
1 tablespoon vegetable oil

Mix marinade. With sharp knife score flank steak by cutting shallow diagonal slices, making diamond design. Place steak in shallow dish and pour marinade over steak. Turn. Cover and refrigerate for 6 hours or overnight. Broil 6 to 8 minutes on each side until desired doneness is reached. Heat remaining marinade and serve with steak, adding extra barbecue sauce if necessary.

Serves 4.

PEPPER STEAKS

2 shell steaks
salt
1 tablespoon freshly ground pepper
2 tablespoons cognac
finely chopped fresh parsley

Sprinkle each side of steaks with salt and press pepper into all sides of steaks with the palm of your hand. Set aside for 15 minutes. Sprinkle a large heavy frying pan lightly with salt. Heat until salt begins to turn brown. Cook steaks until browned on both sides. After turning steaks, lower heat and cook to desired doneness. Remove steaks to serving dish and pour in cognac. Light and pour over steaks. Sprinkle with parsley.

Serves 2.

TOURNEDOS OF BEEF

4 1½-inch-thick slices filet
½ teaspoon salt
4 tablespoons butter
freshly ground pepper
freshly chopped parsley

Tie string around outside of each filet (tournedo) to hold meat in shape. Sprinkle ½ teaspoon of salt in large heavy skillet and heat. When salt begins to brown add steaks and cook over high heat for 5 minutes. Turn steaks and cook for five minutes on this side (10 minutes will produce rare steaks) or until desired doneness. Place pat of butter on each steak and sprinkle liberally with pepper and parsley.

Serves 4.

MARINATED LAMB CHOPS

4 1-inch-thick loin lamb chops
5 tablespoons lemon juice
5 tablespoons olive or vegetable oil
2 cloves garlic, crushed
½ teaspoon dried oregano
salt and pepper to taste

Mix together lemon juice, oil, garlic and oregano in shallow dish large enough to hold 4 chops. Season mixture with salt and pepper. Place chops in sauce and rub generously over both sides. Cover and let marinate for 1 hour at room temperature, turning chops once after first 30 minutes. Broil chops about 5 minutes on each side or until desired doneness.

Serves 2.

Serve with baked potato with sour cream and chopped chives and tomato salad.

SPICY LAMB CHOPS

4 1-inch-thick loin lamb chops
salt and freshly ground pepper
dry mustard
3 tablespoons bacon drippings
1 medium onion, chopped
1 large green pepper, cored, seeded and chopped
½ cup dry white wine
½ cup chicken broth

Sprinkle chops liberally with salt, pepper and dry mustard on both sides. Heat bacon drippings and brown chops on each side. Remove chops to plate and saute onion and green pepper for 5 minutes, stirring occasionally. Return chops to pan. Add wine and broth. Bring to a boil, reduce heat and simmer, covered, for about 50 minutes until chops are tender.

Serves 4

LAMB SHANKS IN DILL SAUCE

4 lamb shanks
salt and pepper
flour
2 tablespoons vegetable oil
2 tablespoons butter
1 medium onion, chopped
1 large clove garlic, crushed
½ teaspoon dried dill weed
2 carrots, scraped and sliced
3 boiled potatoes, cut into quarters
½ cup dry red wine
1 cup beef bouillon

Season lamb shanks with salt and pepper. Coat with flour. Heat oil in large skillet and brown lamb shanks on each side. Place in casserole dish. Add butter to skillet and saute onion and garlic for 5 minutes. Add to casserole with remaining ingredients, cover and bake in preheated 350 F. oven for 1 hour and 15 minutes.

Serves 4.

FRIED PORK CHOPS

4 pork chops, 1-inch thick
salt and freshly ground pepper
Seasoned salt
½ cup flour
3 tablespoons vegetable oil

Season each side of pork chop with salt, pepper and seasoned salt. Dredge in flour. Let chops sit while you heat oil in skillet. Add pork chops and cook over medium low heat for 10 minutes. Turn each chop with spatula. Partially cover, lower heat and cook for 10 minutes. Remove cover and cook 5 minutes until pork chops are tender.

Serves 2.

STUFFED PORK CHOPS

4 1-inch-thick pork chops
4 tablespoons butter
salt and freshly ground pepper to taste
1 stalk celery, finely chopped
2 tablespoons minced onion
1 large Delicious apple, peeled, cored and finely
    chopped
1/3 cup dry white wine or vermouth
1 cup prepared herb stuffing mixture
1/8 teaspoon sage
1/2 cup chicken broth

Melt 2 tablespoons of butter in a large skillet. Season chops with
salt and pepper and brown on both sides in pan. Transfer chops to
side dish and add celery, onion and apple. Saute for about 4 minutes over medium heat, stirring often. Add wine and remaining
butter. Bring to a boil. Sprinkle stuffing mix over pan. Add sage
and stir until mixture is thoroughly moistened. Remove mixture
from pan to bowl and cool. When stuffing mixture has cooled,
divide into four parts. Place one lightly pressed stuffing section on
each chop. Arrange chops in shallow baking pan. Pour broth into
pan and bake in preheated 375 F. oven for 35 minutes.

Serves 4.

PORK SHOULDER WITH LIMA BEANS

4 pork shoulder chops
2 packages frozen lima beans
2 tablespoons butter
salt and pepper
1 medium onion, chopped
1 clove garlic, chopped
1/4 cup brown sugar
1/4 cup wine vinegar
1/2 cup chicken broth

Place lima beans in pan of hot water until they separate easily.
Meanwhile, heat 2 tablespoons butter in large skillet. Season pork

with salt and pepper. Brown meat on both sides. Transfer pork to casserole dish. Add onion and garlic to pan and saute for 4 minutes. Add brown sugar, vinegar, chicken broth and separated and drained lima beans. Stir and pour over pork. Cover casserole and bake in preheated 350 F. oven for 35 to 40 minutes until pork is tender.

Serves 4.

ROAST LOIN OF PORK

3-pound loin of pork
3 tablespoons vegetable oil
1/2 teaspoon dried thyme
1/4 teaspoon salt
freshly ground pepper
1/4 cup red wine
1/4 cup beef stock

Heat oil in skillet and brown roast on all sides. Place roast in roasting pan fat-side-up. Season with thyme, salt and pepper. Insert meat thermometer, and place in preheated 325 F. oven. Combine wine and stock and use to baste roast several times during cooking. Roast pork approximately 30 minutes per pound or until thermometer reaches 185 F. degrees. Let roast rest at least 20 minutes before carving.

Serves 6.

VEAL PICCATA

1 1/2 pounds veal scallops, flattened to 1/4-inch thickness
    with tenderizer mallet
salt and freshly ground pepper
2 tablespoons oil
2 tablespoons butter
2 tablespoons lemon juice
4 tablespoons dry white wine
1 1/2 tablespoons freshly chopped parsley

Wash veal and dry by patting with paper towels. Season each scallop with salt and pepper. Heat oil and butter in large skillet and brown meat over medium high heat on each side, a few pieces at a time. Remove veal to heated serving dish as it is browned. Pour lemon juice and dry white wine into skillet and bring to a boil. Immediately pour over veal and sprinkle with chopped parsley.

Serves 4 to 6.

VEAL RAGOUT

1½ to 2 pounds veal shoulder, cut into 1½-inch cubes
3 tablespoons butter
1 medium onion, finely chopped
1 green pepper, seeded and chopped
2 teaspoons sweet paprika
1 cup peeled and cubed tomatoes
salt and freshly ground pepper to taste
1 8-ounce can tomato sauce
1 cup sour cream

Heat butter in large skillet. Saute veal for about 5 minutes until browned on all sides. Add onion and green pepper and cook 5 minutes, stirring often. Add remaining ingredients, except for sour cream. Combine well, cover and simmer for 1 hour. Remove cover and cook 30 minutes more. Remove from heat and stir in sour cream. Adjust seasoning, if necessary.

Serve with hot cooked buttered noodles.

Serves 4 to 6.

WIENER SCHNITZEL

4 boneless veal cutlets, flattened with meat tenderizer
*   mallet*
salt and freshly ground pepper to taste
flour
2 eggs, beaten
bread crumbs
½ cup vegetable oil

Season chops with salt and pepper. Dust with flour. Dip in beaten eggs and coat with bread crumbs. Heat oil in large skillet and brown veal on each side. Serve with lemon wedges.

To make "A La Holstein," top each piece of cooked veal with a fried egg.

Serves 4.

FISH AND SHELLFISH

Seafood is, in many ways, the ideal food. It is easy to buy and cook fish. Fish is filled with vital nutrients and is not fattening. Waste is minimal—no fat or heavy bones. Shellfish, of course, do have shells to be discarded.

Fresh fish is always best. So, become friends with your local fishmonger, and have him help you decide on the best fish available each day.

Cooking methods for fish vary, but most are simple. Fish cooks quickly, so above all adhere to suggested cooking times. There is no rare, medium or well-done. Fish is done when it is opaque. Overcooking will produce dry, tasteless fish.

When buying fish look for these characteristics: full, bright, bulging eyes; red gills that are free of slime; flesh that is firm to the touch; shiny skin and scales that adhere tightly to the fish. There must be no objectionable odor. If buying filets or steaks, look for firm moist pieces with no brown or yellow edges.

The following forms and cuts are available in fish markets:

Filets: Boneless pieces of fish cut lengthwise from sides of fish away from back bone.

Steaks: Pieces of fish which are cross sections of a large dressed fish, about 1-inch thick.

Dressed: A fish that has been cleaned, its scales, entrails, fins, head and tail removed.

Drawn: A fish that has had its entrails removed.

Whole: A fish as it comes from the water. It must be cleaned (scaled and entrails removed) before cooking.

The portions you serve will depend on the individual's appetite, but usually ⅓ pound of fish filet or steak is enough for one. Allow ½ pound per person for a dressed fish. I don't recommend frozen fish, because the taste is greatly affected by the freezing process.

Shellfish and mollusks are great delicacies. When selecting live lobsters or crabs make sure they show active signs of life. Oysters, clams and mussels usually close their shells when lightly tapped. It is possible to purchase partially prepared shellfish: oysters, clams, scallops and mussels which have been removed from their shells and are ready to be either eaten or cooked. Shrimp heads have been removed before they reach the market in this country. You can buy them in their shells or shelled. However, you will pay dearly if your fish man shells them for you.

If you buy frozen shellfish, make sure the package is tightly wrapped with no bulging sides. The bulge means that the package had thawed at some point and had then been refrozen, and this results in waterlogged, grainy flesh with all the flavor gone.

Shellfish usually refers to both crustaceans and mollusks. Crustaceans are lobsters, crabs and shrimps and mollusks are oysters, clams, mussels and scallops.

There are two types of clams: hard shell and soft shell. Hard-shell clams are usually eaten raw and on the half shell. Medium-size hard-shell clams are called cherrystone. The smallest ones are called littleneck. The large clams or chowder clams are chopped and used in soups and chowders. Soft-shell clams have a thin shell and a long neck. They are always cooked, usually steamed, before eating.

To open hard-shell clams rinse them in cold water several times. Then let them stand in cold lightly salted water for several minutes. Drain and insert a clam knife or strong thin blade between shells near the thick end and turn blade across shell until muscle holding the shell together is cut. Once opened, retain as much liquid in the side of shell containing the clam as possible.

There are soft and hard-shelled crab too. Hard-shell crabs, such as the blue crabs from the East coast, should be cooked alive. Steam them in a little salted water for 7 to 8 minutes and allow them to cool. Pull back shell, remove gills and face of crab. The eyes and sandbag should come off easily with shell. Break body in half so you can remove meat. Then crack claws and extract meat.

Soft-shell crabs are crabs that have shed their old hard shell and have been caught during the roughly forty-eight hours that it takes to grow a new one. To clean soft-shell crabs, remove spongy material under the pointed sections and the feathery gills on each side. Cut across the front of the crab to remove eyes and sandbag.

Oysters, which are considered a great delicacy by many food lovers, are not difficult to shuck, but the task requires both strength and experience. Scrub the oyster under cold running water with a stiff brush. Hold oyster flat-side-up on a thick cloth in the palm of your hand. Have the hinged end facing you. With a pair of pliers break off thin end of shell. Discard flat shell and release oyster from shell with a small sharp knife.

GEOFFREY HOLDER'S RED SNAPPER PARAMIN KENDAL *

Geoffrey Holder, the talented dancer, choreographer, actor and painter is also an accomplished cook. His Caribbean Cookbook is filled with imaginative recipes and his own illustrations. When I asked him advice for men for this book he quickly allowed, "Men had better start cooking in this day of women's liberation, or they will suffer."

> 4 pounds red snapper
> 1½ cloves garlic, minced
> ½ teaspoon Accent
> 1 teaspoon salt
> black pepper to taste
> 1 ounce rum
> 2 teaspoons thyme (½ teaspoon dried)
> 2 teaspoons shallots, chopped fine
> 1 cup oil
> 1½ cups onions, minced
> 2 tablespoons celery, chopped fine
> ½ teaspoon parsley, minced
> 1 teaspoon oregano
> 1 teaspoon rosemary
> 2 teaspoons chives, chopped
> 2 tablespoons butter
> 1 cup white wine
> 1 tablespoon Worcestershire sauce
> 1 teaspoon sugar
> 1 teaspoon cornstarch

Season the red snapper with minced garlic, Accent, salt and pepper to taste, rum, 1 teaspoon of the thyme, and the chopped shallots. Marinate for 1 hour. Then drain and fry (about 8 to 10 minutes) in hot oil until skin is crisp. Remove and drain the fish on paper towels.

Combine onions, celery, parsley, oregano, rosemary, the remaining thyme, and chives. Sautee this mixture in butter (8 to 10 minutes) until onions are tender. Then add wine, Worcestershire sauce, sugar, and 1 cup water. Simmer for 10 minutes.

Then place fish in the pan with sauce, cover, and cook on low flame for 10 minutes. Turn fish on other side, cover, and cook again for another 10 minutes. Remove fish and place on serving dish.

Thicken sauce with 1 teaspoon cornstarch dissolved in 1 tablespoon water. Pour over fish and serve.

POACHED RED SNAPPER FILETS

4 filets of red snapper
1 cup water
¾ cup dry white wine
1 tablespoon chopped shallots
1 stalk celery, chopped
1 carrot, sliced
salt to taste
4 peppercorns

Butter bottom of skillet and add filets and remaining ingredients. Cover and simmer for 15 minutes. Transfer filets to heated serving platter and serve with Mousseline Sauce (see index for recipe).

Serves 4.

BOILED SHRIMP

Here is the basic recipe for boiled shrimp to be used in salads or other dishes as needed.

> 3 cups water
> 1 small onion, quartered
> 1 teaspoon lemon juice
> ½ teaspoon salt
> freshly ground pepper to taste
> 1 pound shrimp, shelled and deveined

In a large saucepan, place all ingredients except for shrimp and bring to a boil. Add shrimp, reduce heat and simmer for about 5 minutes until shrimp are pink. Drain.

> Serves 4.

DEEP-FRIED BUTTERFLIED SHRIMP

> 2 pounds large raw shrimp
> flour
> 2 eggs, lightly breaten
> bread crumbs
> 3 cups vegetable oil
> salt and freshly ground pepper

Shell and devein shrimp, but leave tails intact. Cut each shrimp lengthwise, but don't cut all the way through. Flatten slightly and coat each side with flour, then egg and finally with bread crumbs. Heat oil to 375 F. in large saucepan and cook a few shrimp at a time for about 5 minutes until golden. Remove with tongs and drain. Season with salt and pepper.

Delicious with cold beer.

> Serves 4.

SHRIMP CURRY

1 pound boiled shrimp
3 tablespoons butter
3 tablespoons flour
1 tablespoon curry powder
1 cup milk
1/2 cup heavy cream
1/2 teaspoon salt
white pepper
fresh chopped parsley

Heat butter in saucepan and stir in flour and curry powder. Cook 1 minute over medium heat. Heat milk and cream in another pan. Slowly pour milk and cream into butter sauce, whisking constantly until thickened. Add salt and white pepper to taste. Then, add shrimp. Simmer for 5 minutes. Serve over rice and sprinkle with parsley.

Serves 4.

SHRIMP SCAMPI

1 1/2 pounds raw medium shrimp, shelled and deveined
1/2 cup olive oil
2 cloves garlic, crushed
2 tablespoons freshly chopped parsley
1 tablespoon lemon juice
1/2 teaspoon salt
freshly ground pepper to taste

In bowl mix all ingredients except for shrimp. Add shrimp, cover and marinate for at least 1 hour in refrigerator. Place shrimp in greased shallow pan. Broil for 5 minutes. Turn each shrimp, baste with marinade, and cook for a moment more until golden. Garnish with lemon wedges.

Serve with Risotto Milanese (see index for recipe), green salad and chilled dry white wine.

Serves 4.

BOILED LOBSTER

4 1½-pound lobsters
½ pound butter

Cover bottom of large pot with 1-inch of boiling water. Place live lobsters in pot, cover and bring to a boil and cook for about 15 minutes. Remove lobsters and when cool enough to handle, place lobsters on their backs. With a long, strong, sharp knife, split lobsters in half lengthwise. Remove small sac near the head and vein running the length of lobster. Serve little bowls of melted butter.

Serves 4.

VINCENT SARDI'S POACHED SCROD
À LA PAISANA WITH HOLLANDAISE SAUCE
OR HOT MAYONNAISE

Here is one of Vincent Sardi's personal favorites, which is served in his famous restaurant.

4 6-ounce filets of Boston scrod
1 tablespoon fine chopped onion
1 tablespoon finely chopped celery
1 tablespoon finely chopped tomato
1 teaspoon fresh chopped parsley
salt and pepper to taste
1 bay leaf
1 pinch of thyme
1 cup fish stock or 1 cup water
1 lemon

Place filets in skillet. Sprinkle with onion, celery, tomato, parsley, salt and pepper, bay leaf and thyme. Pour in fish stock or water and juice of lemon. Cover and cook over medium heat until fish is white and flakes easily, about 12 minutes.

Serve with Hollandaise Sauce or hot mayonnaise.

Serves 4.

GOUJONNETTES OF SOLE

1½ pounds sole filets, cut into ½- by 2½-inch strips
flour
3 eggs, lightly beaten
3 cups dried bread crumbs
3 cups vegetable oil
salt and freshly ground pepper to taste

Dredge fish pieces with flour, then beaten eggs. Roll in bread crumbs and fry a few pieces at a time in hot oil until golden. This will take only a few minutes. Drain on paper towels. Season with salt and pepper and pile on cloth-lined heated serving dish as cooked. Serve immediately with lemon wedges, parsley and tartar sauce.

Serves 4.

SOLE MEUNIÈRE

Sole Meunière is a simple and quick way to cook sole or other fish filets. It's rarely done properly, however, in restaurants or at home. The delicate flavor of the sole should be the predominant flavor with light overtones of butter and lemon.

4 6-ounce sole filets
salt and pepper
flour
5 tablespoons butter or as needed
1 tablespoon lemon juice
1 tablespoon freshly chopped parsley

Season filets with salt and pepper. Lightly coat with flour. Heat 2 tablespoons butter in large skillet and saute fish until golden and crisp on each side. Add butter as needed. Carefully transfer to heated serving platter. Add 3 tablespoons butter to skillet and cook until it begins to brown. Immediately add lemon juice and parsley. Stir and pour over filets. Serve at once.

Serve with boiled potatoes.

Serves 4.

CHARLES DOBSON'S SOFT-SHELL CRABS

Charles Dobson is the owner of Charlie's and Dobson's restaurants in New York City.

One of Charles' happy memories of his childhood in East Virginia was accompanying his grandfather to the shore and watching crabs shed their shells in wooden floats. The soft-shell crabs were quickly collected and packed in seaweed and shipped to markets. Charles' recipe is classic and he suggests you serve the sauteed soft-shell crabs with tartar sauce and plenty of cold beer.

> 12 soft-shell crabs
> salt and pepper
> flour
> 3 tablespoons butter
> 2 tablespoons vegetable oil

Have your fish man clean your crabs. They must be cooked the same day. Season them with salt and pepper and lightly coat with flour. Heat butter and oil and saute crabs, a few at a time, until golden on each side.

> Serves 4.

COLD POACHED TROUT

> 2 quarts water
> 2 stalks celery, chopped
> 2 carrots, chopped
> 2 sprigs parsley
> 1 bay leaf
> ¼ teaspoon dried thyme
> 6 peppercorns
> 2 slices lemon
> ½ cup dry white wine
> 4 rainbow trout, cleaned

First prepare a Court Bouillon by placing all ingredients except for trout in saucepan, bringing to a boil, reducing heat to a simmer and cooking for 30 minutes. Strain. Place trout in buttered baking dish with 2½-inch sides. Pour Court Bouillon over trout. Cover dish with foil. Bake in preheated 350 F. oven for 20 minutes. Remove dish from oven and let trout cool in broth. Carefully remove trout to serving dish, cover and chill thoroughly. Just before serving remove top skin of each trout, which is easy to do with a small sharp knife. Sprinkle trout with lemon and serve with tartar sauce.

Serves 4.

JUDGE VINCENT COMMISSA'S BAKED FRESH HADDOCK

Judge Vincent Commissa of Newark, New Jersey, inherited his interest in food and cooking skills from his mother, Consiglia, who was born in a little town north of Naples. Judge Commissa reminisces over his mother's escarole pie made with pine nuts, black olives, olive oil and seasonings baked in a thick dough; her superb breads; her sponge cake. But most of all her delicate zucchini blossoms or flowers that she cooked in three ways: coated in a light batter and fried; shaped into patties and sauteed; or unopened and stemmed, then dipped briefly into boiling water seasoned with salt, pepper and lemon juice. "The zucchini blossoms melted in your mouth. Mother could never pile up a plate with sauteed zucchini blossom patties. They disappeared too quickly."

Judge Commissa thinks zucchini is the world's greatest vegetable and grows it in enormous quantities in his large backyard garden along with oak lettuce, peppers, tomatoes, broccoli, basil and other vegetables and herbs. He won't eat supermarket-bought ingredients for salads, claiming that "They are tasteless vehicles for commercial dressings." And on the subject of salad dressings, he urges mixing them at home, the simpler the better: oil, lemon juice, salt and pepper." Only eat vegetables and fruits in season," Judge Commissa advises. Each year he eagerly anticipates the fall for tender juicy Comice pears to arrive from California. "They are only good if you bite into them and juice runs over your hand." He thinks Bartlett and Bosc pears are hand grenades.

Judge Commissa has been making his Baked Fresh Haddock dish for over 25 years and cautions, "The wine you cook with should be as good as the wine you drink." He recommends a Premier or Grand Cru Chablis for his recipe.

    4 6-ounce haddock filets
    salt and pepper
    Italian-style bread crumbs
    1 medium onion, thinly sliced
    2 tablespoons butter
    ½ cup dry white wine

Season filets with salt and pepper. Coat with bread crumbs. Place
in lightly greased baking dish large enough to comfortably hold
fish. Filets should not touch each other. Place onion slices on top
of filets and dot with equal amounts of butter. Pour wine around
filets and place in preheated 375 F. oven. Bake for 20 minutes.

    Serves 4.

SAUTEED SCALLOPS

    1½ pounds bay scallops
    salt and pepper
    flour
    2 eggs, beaten
    6 tablespoons butter
    2 tablespoons vegetable oil

Season scallops with salt and pepper. Dust with flour. Dip each
scallop into beaten eggs and roll in bread crumbs. Heat 3 tablespoons butter and 1 tablespoon oil in skillet and saute scallops
several at a time. Add more butter and oil as needed. As scallops
are cooked, drain.

  Serve with green peas and boiled potatoes. Garnish with lemon
wedges.

    Serves 4.

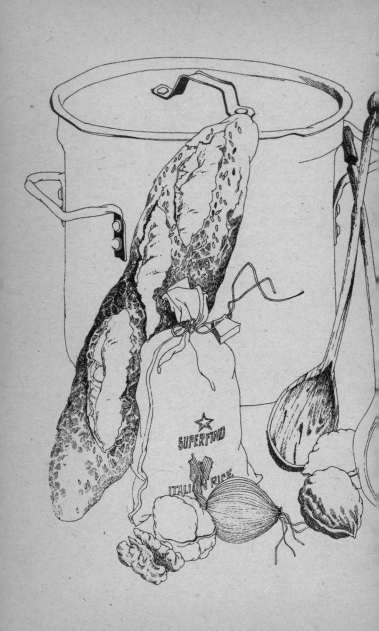

chapter 8 · pastas

If by some stroke of good fortune I could have anything I wanted, it wouldn't be a sable coat or a Rolls Royce, it would be an airline ticket to Venice and dinner at Harry's Bar. Dinner would begin with their exquisite Tagliatelle Verdi Gratinate (or homemade green noodles). The noodles melt in your mouth like butter and the delicious creamy béchamel sauce with meat is sublime. Once you've tasted a magnificently prepared pasta dish your palate will never forget it. But you don't have to go to Italy to find one. Perfect pasta can be prepared in your own kitchen.

Pasta is the biggest selling food of Italian origin manufactured in the United States. Most of us immediately associate pasta with spaghetti and macaroni, but there are many different types of pasta to choose from: rigatoni, linguini, lasagne, giant shells, vermicelli, ditali, fedelini, ravioli, tortellini, tagliatelle, manicotti and ziti, to name a few. Whatever its shape and size, pasta is composed of specially ground durum wheat and water. Sometimes eggs are added. It is a very healthy food. Even factory-produced pasta is generally very good because it is a simple food hard to downgrade. When we are served a poor dish of pasta in a restaurant or at home, it is because it hasn't been cooked or drained properly, or because it is covered with too much sauce or one that is inferior.

Regardless of the shape and size, all good pasta tastes pretty much the same, it's the sauce that makes the difference. The large sizes of pasta such as rigatoni or shells need a thicker sauce, while the smaller sizes, vermicelli or fedelini, for instance, require a thinner, more delicate sauce. The sauce can range from the simple tomato or marinara to the superb Northern Italian specialty, pesto sauce, which I have included.

Here are a few helpful suggestions for successful pasta dishes. One pound of pasta (enough for four people) should be cooked in a large pot holding 6 to 7 quarts of rapidly boiling water with 1 tablespoon of both salt and oil added. The oil helps to keep the pasta from sticking to itself. Stir the pasta with a long-handled wooden spoon or fork occasionally during cooking time to further prevent sticking. Cooking time for various pastas differs. Use the package directions as a guide, but since they generally suggest a minute or two too much cooking, you must test it by taste toward the end of cooking time. It is generally agreed pasta is best when cooked al dente (to the tooth) or just until tender. Overcooking produces limp, soft pasta.

When it is cooked, quickly drain pasta in a large colander. Shake the colander and, if the pasta is the tube kind, lift it with spoons or forks to help get rid of the hidden water inside. Place pasta in a large heated bowl or serving dish and immediately pour about 3 tablespoons of melted butter over pasta and toss, unless the sauce is composed mainly of butter. Next, add sauce and toss again, coating each piece. Check seasoning and serve.

BEN PAGLIAROLI'S LINGUINI AGLIO OLIO

From the moment you enter my Aunt Angela and Uncle Ben's house in Mountainside, New Jersey, until you leave, their table is filled with food. They have a happy house which is usually full of relatives. There's singing and dancing and card playing and never a dull moment. Late in the evening after people have gone home or to bed, my uncle, cousin Tom and I spend a peaceful time together. We feast on leftovers, cold cuts, vegetables and cakes, groan in unison and go to bed. None of us ever has a hard time falling asleep either.

This is my Uncle Ben's favorite recipe, and he tells why: "Almost everyone enjoys pasta, no matter what size or shape. But personally, my favorite is Linguini Aglio Olio (garlic and oil), first served to me in my younger days in a little town in Italy. It's particularly satisfying after a night of hearty drinking and poker playing and so easy to prepare that everyone can get into the act. I don't know where in Italy this dish originated, but I suspect it is Southern Italy. I consider it a man's dish, but not being a male chauvinist, I invite the women to try it!"

> ¾ cup olive oil
> 7 large cloves of fresh garlic, chopped fine
> 1 can anchovies
> 1 pound linguini
> Parmesan cheese, freshly grated
> salt
> freshly ground pepper
> red pepper seeds

Heat water in a large kettle to cook linguini. Follow directions on package for amount of water and salt. Heat oil in saucepan until it is hot but not smoking. Add garlic, lower heat and cook garlic until it starts to turn color. Add anchovies and cook, stirring until anchovies break apart. Remove from heat. When the linguini water starts to boil, dip out 1 cup of water and add to the garlic and oil mixture, cover and keep hot over low heat until linguini is cooked. Drain linguini and transfer to deep serving dish. Add half of sauce, toss and pour remainder of sauce over pasta.

Garnish with freshly grated Parmesan cheese, black and red pepper.

Serves 4.

RISOTTO MILANESE

Risotto Milanese is not a pasta dish, but I place it in this section because it is an important Italian starch dish.

> 6 tablespoons butter
> 2 tablespoons finely chopped onion
> 1 cup long-grain rice
> 1 cup dry white wine
> 1 cup beef broth
> ¼ teaspoon salt
> freshly grated pepper to tusle
> freshly grated Parmesan cheese

Heat butter in skillet and add onion. Saute for 3 or 4 minutes, stirring. Add rice and stir for several minutes. Heat wine and stock and pour over rice. Add salt and pepper, cover and cook over low heat for about 20 minutes until rice is tender.

Serve with extra grated Parmesan cheese.

Serves 4 to 6.

RISOTTO MILANESE WITH SHRIMP:

To make Risotto Milanese With Shrimp follow above recipe and add 1 cup chopped raw shrimp, 1 chopped scallion and ½ cup fresh peas 5 minutes before end of cooking time. Stir and serve immediately with crusty bread and white wine.

FETTUCCINE ALFREDO

8 ounces fettucini noodles
1 stick sweet butter, melted
½ cup freshly grated Parmesan cheese
⅔ cup heavy cream
salt and greshly ground pepper to taste

Cook noodles according to package directions. Drain well in colander. Turn into serving dish, add butter and cheese. Toss. Add cream and sprinkle generously with salt and pepper. Toss and serve.

Serve with broiled Italian sausage, a green salad and chilled white wine.

Serves 4.

ITALIAN SAUSAGE IN DOUGH

The following dish makes a handsome meal served with scrambled eggs and hash brown potatoes.

8 Italian sweet sausages
1 package hot roll mix
2 egg yolks, beaten

Bake sausages in baking dish in 375 F. oven until browned. Prick sausages with fork in several places so they won't explode. When cooked, cool on paper towels. Meanwhile, prepare dough according to package directions. After the first rise, push dough down and divide into 8 pieces. Roll each piece out on a little flour into rectangular shape about 6 by 4 inches. Wrap sausage in dough. Secure dough by pressing edges together. Place on greased baking sheet seam-side-down and let rise for 15 minutes. Brush with egg yolk and bake in preheated 350 F. oven for 15 minutes or until golden.

Serves 4.

LASAGNE

Lasagne is a perfect party dish. It can be prepared in advance and
warmed up just before serving. Accompany with mixed salad,
Italian bread and plenty of red wine.

> 3 Italian sausages, removed from casings
> 1 pound ground beef
> 1 medium onion, chopped
> 1 clove garlic, minced
> ½ teaspoon dried oregano
> ½ teaspoon salt
> freshly ground pepper to taste
> 3½ cups tomato sauce
> 1 pound lasagne noodles
> 1 pound ricotta cheese
> 1 pound mozzarella cheese
> 8 ounces grated Parmesan cheese

Brown sausage in skillet and drain. Brown ground beef, onion and
garlic until meat is no longer pink, stirring occasionally. Add sausage, oregano, salt, pepper and tomato sauce. Combine. Simmer
while noodles are cooking. Cook lasagne noodles according to
package directions. Drain. In rectangular baking dish about
2½-inches deep, cover bottom lightly with sauce. Line with 1
layer of noodles, placed in rows. Place several spoonfuls of ricotta
cheese along each noodle. Top with thin slices of mozzarella.
Spoon sauce over cheese and sprinkle liberally with Parmesan
cheese. Top with lasagne noodles and repeat process, ending up
with noodles topped with sauce, mozzarella and Parmesan cheese.
Bake in preheated 350 F. oven for 35 minutes.

Serves 6 or 8

SPAGHETTI CARBONARA

12 strips bacon
8 ounces spaghetti
2 eggs, beaten
salt and pepper
4 tablespoons melted butter
½ cup cooked green peas
1 scallion, finely chopped
3 tablespoons Parmesan cheese
1 tablespoon fresh chopped parsley

Sautee bacon until crisp, drain and crumble. Set aside. Bring large pot of lightly salted water to a boil. Add spaghetti and cook for 7 to 8 minutes until just done (al dente). Place in serving dish and immediately pour eggs, which have been seasoned with salt and pepper, and melted butter over hot spaghetti. Toss. The hot spaghetti cooks the eggs. Add bacon and remaining ingredients. Toss and serve immediately.

Serves 4.

WINFIELD LEVI'S SPAGHETTI

The Winfield Levis' summer home is a 40-foot Viking Sporting Fisherman. Win and his wife Joyce have found that certain food products are especially handy on boats: minute rice, pasta, canned ham, dried or canned soups, Bisquick, garlic dry salad mix and wine; all storageable items. An electric crock pot and frying pan are helpful, too. The kitchen on their boat has a full refrigerator, range with oven and a dining room table. The table, when covered with cushions, becomes a comfortable bed. I know, because I've slept on the table, after a feast of Win's spaghetti.

8 ounces spaghetti
4 tablespoons olive or vegetable oil
4 tablespoons melted butter
½ package Good Seasons garlic dry salad mix

Cook spaghetti according to package directions. Drain in colander. Place in serving bowl and add oil and butter. Toss until well coated with mixture. Sprinkle garlic mix over spaghetti and toss again.

Serve with mixed salad, Italian bread and chilled white wine.

Serves 4.

AL PESTO SAUCE FOR
SPAGHETTI OR LINGUINI

2 cloves garlic, peeled and chopped
½ cup chopped fresh basil
3 ounces cream cheese
⅔ cup olive oil
salt and pepper
½ cup grated Parmesan cheese
1 pound spaghetti or linguini

Crush garlic with basil with mortar and pestle. Add cream cheese little bits at a time. When thoroughly mixed, slowly pour in olive oil and continue mixing. This process can be done in a blender. Season with a little salt and plenty of freshly ground pepper. Finally, add grated Parmesan cheese. The mixture should be the consistency of a thick sauce. Cook pasta in boiling salted water, al dente. Drain. Place in platter and pour sauce over pasta. Toss well. Sprinkle extra grated Parmesan cheese over each serving.

Serves 4 to 6.

MARINARA SAUCE

¼ cup olive or vegetable oil
1 medium onion, chopped
2 cloves garlic, minced (optional)
½ teaspoon dried basil
1 tablespoon fresh chopped parsley
3 cups fresh peeled and chopped tomatoes (canned to-
*   matoes can be used as substitute)*
1 cup tomato sauce
½ teaspoon salt
freshly ground pepper to taste

Heat oil in large heavy saucepan and saute onion and garlic for 4 or 5 minutes, stirring occasionally. Add remaining ingredients, bring to a boil, reduce heat and simmer for 1 hour, stirring once or twice during cooking time.

Serve with your favorite pasta and freshly grated Parmesan cheese.

Serves 4 to 6.

MICHELE'S MEAT SAUCE

2 Italian sweet sausages, meat removed from casings
1 pound ground beef
3 tablespoons olive oil
1 medium onion, finely chopped
1 clove garlic, minced
3½ cups canned Italian plum tomatoes and sauce (chop tomatoes)
1 8-ounce can tomato sauce
1 beef bouillon cube
3 tablespoons tomato puree
½ teaspoon dried basil
½ teaspoon fennel seeds
1 tablespoon fresh chopped parsley
½ teaspoon salt
freshly ground pepper
½ cup red wine

In large skillet saute sausage meat and ground beef until no longer pink in color, stirring often. Drain well. In large heavy saucepan heat oil and saute onion and garlic for 5 minutes. Add sausage and ground beef mixture and remaining ingredients. Bring to a boil, reduce heat and simmer for 1 hour, stirring occasionally.

Serves 4 to 6.

PORTO FINO'S CREAMY WALNUT SAUCE WITH PASTA

¾ cup chopped walnuts
1 clove garlic, crushed
⅔ cup ricotta cheese
¼ cup fresh grated Parmesan cheese
1 tablespoon fresh chopped parsley
½ teaspoon salt
freshly ground pepper to taste
½ cup olive oil

Place walnuts and garlic in blender or food processor and grind to fine. Add remaining ingredients except for olive oil and puree for 10 seconds. Pour in olive oil slowly and mix well.

Pour sauce over 8 ounces hot cooked pasta, such as spaghetti or fettuccine.

Serves 4 as a first course.

Chapter 9. breads heros and other sandwiches

BREADS

Slicing a loaf of fresh homemade bread, smearing it with butter and eating it right off the board is a wonderfully satisfying treat. Especially if you have baked the bread yourself.

Bread making is not difficult and a lot of men have recently discovered the pleasures of kneading and braiding and baking it. A good way to begin is to bake a few quick breads (to give yourself the old "success experience") and then progress to yeast breads. Once you are confident of your ability as a baker you might want to do several loaves at a time and then freeze the extra loaves until they are needed.

A loaf of your own special bread makes a perfect host-hostess gift. It is received with surprise, delight and much more enthusiasm than the usual wine or flowers.

QUICK BANANA NUT BREAD

1¾ cups all-purpose flour
1 teaspoon baking soda
½ teaspoon baking powder
¾ cup sugar
½ cup vegetable oil
½ teaspoon grated lemon rind
2 eggs, lightly beaten
1 cup mashed ripe banana pulp (2 large bananas)
½ cup chopped walnuts

Combine flour, soda and baking powder in large mixing bowl. Blend together sugar, oil and lemon rind. Mix well with flour mixture. Add eggs and banana pulp. Thoroughly combine. Stir in nuts. Turn batter into greased 9 by 5 by 3-inch bread pan and bake in preheated 350 F. oven for 1 hour.

QUICK OATMEAL BREAD

TOPPING:

2 tablespoons light brown sugar, firmly packed
2 tablespoons finely chopped pecans
¼ teaspoon cinnamon

BREAD:

1¼ cups sifted flour
¾ cup sugar
1 teaspoon salt
1 teaspoon baking powder
1 teaspoon baking soda
½ teaspoon cinnamon
¼ teaspoon nutmeg
1 cup quick-cooking oats
½ cup raisins
1¼ cups sweetened applesauce
⅓ cup vegetable oil
2 eggs
¼ cup milk

First, prepare topping: In small bowl mix together brown sugar, chopped pecans and cinnamon. Set aside. In large mixing bowl combine flour, sugar, salt, baking powder, baking soda, cinnamon and nutmeg. Then stir in oats and raisins. In another bowl mix applesauce, oil, eggs and milk. Pour into flour and oat mixture and mix thoroughly. Grease a 9 by 5 by 3-inch loaf pan. Add a tablespoon of flour and shake over greased surface of pan. Pour bread mixture into pan and cover with topping. Bake in preheated 350 F. oven for about 55 minutes or until loaf is done. Test for doneness by inserting wooden toothpick or cake tester in center of loaf. If it comes out clean, bread is done. Cool bread in pan or wire rack for about 10 minutes. Loosen edges with small spatula and turn out bread. Cool completely on rack and wrap in plastic wrap for 6 hours before cutting.

PAT FOX'S WHOLE WHEAT BREAD

Pat Fox is an actor from Montana who lives in New York City. He's a bread lover and I'm hooked on his whole wheat bread. "This recipe was my grandmother's, but my mother perfected it. She used to air mail me a couple of loaves a month until I noticed that the stamps were about $2 a throw. I decided to break down and learn how to do it myself. It makes the best toast in the world. And, by the way, if you use the same measuring cup for your laundry, as I do, be sure to wash out all the soap first."

> 3½ cups whole wheat flour (must be coarse like graham-brand flour)
> 3½ cups white unbleached flour
> 1 tablespoon salt
> 1 cup lukewarm water
> 1 teaspoon sugar
> 1 package dry yeast
> 1¾ cups warm water
> 2 tablespoons honey

Mix all dry ingredients in a large bowl and form a crater in the center. In a small bowl put water, sugar and yeast. Stir until yeast has dissolved. Into another bowl put warm water and 2 tablespoons honey and stir. Pour both water mixtures into crater of dry ingredients and stir until liquid in center is thickened but is the consistency of a batter. About 1½ cups of flour has been incorporated into the liquid. This is the sponge and starts the yeast working. Cover and let sit for ½ hour. Now, finish stirring and mixing dough together. Knead dough for about 10 minutes until smooth. Shape into 2 loaves and place in greased or Teflon bread loaf pans. Cover and let sit for 1 hour. Bake in preheated 450 F. oven for 15 minutes. Reduce heat to 350 and bake for 45 minutes more.

Yield: 2 loaves.

INGA'S DANISH BREAD

1 egg
1 cup dark brown sugar
1 cup sour milk*
2 cups flour
1 teaspoon baking soda
½ teaspoon baking powder
½ cup Grape-nuts

Mix together egg and brown sugar. Add sour milk and beat well. Add remaining ingredients and beat about 100 strokes. Turn into greased loaf pan. Bake in preheated 350 F. oven for about 50 minutes. Let cool 30 minutes before slicing.

Makes excellent toast.

AUDREY'S MEXICAN CORN BREAD

1 8-ounce package cream cheese, at room temperature
2 eggs, lightly beaten
1 cup corn meal
1 tablespoon baking powder
½ teaspoon salt
1 8-ounce can creamed corn
8 ounces grated Cheddar cheese

Cream the cream cheese into the lightly beaten eggs. Mix all other ingredients and add to cream cheese mixture. Stir until well blended. Pour into buttered 10-inch heavy iron skillet or skillet with metal handle. Bake in preheated 335 F. oven for about 45 minutes.

*Milk can be soured by adding 1 tablespoon white vinegar and letting it sit for 5 minutes.

GEORGE BALASSES' CHALLAH

"If I'd stayed with General Motors, I'd probably not have become its president, though Pete Estes, a classmate and frat brother, did. On the other hand, I doubt that Pete has time to bake bread—which I can do any morning, afternoon or evening. I've had several careers, but while I was working as a public relations expert in New York city, my wife Teda (a market research field director) and I visited Amagansett, Long Island, for a summer weekend. While we were there we decided that Amagansett needed an antique shop. So we opened that shop, changing careers once again, but this time gaining time to cook and bake.

"When I discovered that my mother-in-law loved challah bread (which is similar to the Greek bread my mother used to bake), I baked a loaf for her. I've had a steady customer ever since. In fact, for many years I've baked all the bread we eat. Challah is easy to bake and easy to eat. To achieve the tender but chewy quality that makes the bread so delicious, the dough should rise three times: a big chunk of time.

"However, one needn't become a slave to the bread-baking cycle. The cycle can be stretched and bent to one's own schedule, without loss of bread quality.

"I can, for instance, bake at 9 or 10 in the evening without staying up for the five consecutive hours.

"I mix the dough and knead it well. Very important to spend 10 to 15 minutes pushing and turning the mass until it comes to life. It's easy to recognize this stage. Jab 2 fingers into the dough, withdraw and the dough quickly fills out again.

"Next, the dough is placed in a greased large rising pan and deposited in the refrigerator or any cold (but not freezing) place. At our house we have a stairway leading to an unheated upstairs. Temperature on the steps in winter is 45 to 50 degrees. Refrigerators are usually in the 40 to 50 degrees range. Both temperatures are okay for bread rising.

"Yeast works at any temperature from 120 down to freezing, when it stops until thawed out. Above 120 F. kills yeast. When placing the pan, allow space around and above it for overflow. Even if you're away a long time, rambling dough can be neatly shoved back in place and punched down for the next rise. From experience, I've learned that 3 or 4 hours in a cool place equal one hour in normal temperature. Check dough and push down when double in volume.

"After two risings, shape the dough and place in baking pan; fill it to slightly over the half-way mark.

"The final pre-bake rise can be done in a cool spot if a 3 to 4 hour wait is desired, or it can take place in a normal room temperature. However, if the dough is cold, allow about 2 hours for the final rise, to just above the edge of pan. I seldom follow the same recipe twice, because I don't measure ingredients, except by eye. But here's a recipe that I started with when I did measure."

> 2 packages dry yeast
> 1½ cups warm water (approximately 110 F.)
> ⅓ cup corn oil
> ⅓ cup honey
> 3 eggs, beaten
> 1 tablespoon coarse salt or 1 teaspoon regular salt
> 2 pinches saffron
> 6 to 7 cups unbleached white flour
> 2 egg yolks, beaten
> ½ teaspoon poppy seeds

Dissolve yeast in warm water in large bowl (about 5 minutes). With wooden spoon, stir in oil, honey, eggs, salt and saffron. Next, add half flour and stir well. Gradually add another 2 cups of flour, mixing dough until it begins to come away from the sides of the bowl. Turn dough onto well-floured surface and knead, adding remaining flour. Kneading will take at least 10 minutes. Dough is ready when it is smooth and elastic and stops taking flour. Place dough in large greased bowl. Turn once so top surface is oiled. Cover with cloth and let rise until doubled in size. In warm place, rising will take about 1 hour, 2 hours or longer in cooler areas. Punch down and allow to rise until doubled again. Punch down again and divide into 6 equal parts. Roll each piece with palms to form a cylinder about 12 inches long. Braid 3 pieces together to form a loaf and place on greased baking sheet. Repeat for second loaf. Allow to rise until doubled. (Dough may also be placed in oiled bread pans without braiding.) Brush bread with egg yolks and dust with poppy seeds. Bake in preheated 400 F. oven for 10 minutes. Lower heat to 350 F. and continue to bake for 35 minutes, until well-browned.

Makes 2 loaves.

GEORGE BALASSES' BISCUITS

"The easiest and fastest bread I make is the biscuit. For a dozen biscuits I use buttermilk or yoghurt," George explains.

> 2 cups flour or more if needed to thicken
> 1 teaspoon salt
> ½ teaspoon baking soda
> 1½ teaspoons baking powder
> ¾ cup yoghurt or buttermilk
> 1 egg
> ¼ cup vegetable oil, lard or butter

Place flour, salt, baking soda and baking powder in large bowl. Add remaining ingredients. Stir it well until dough comes away from sides of the bowl. Then knead it a little until it holds together. Pat or roll dough out to about ¼ inch thick. Cut into squares with knife or circles with cookie cutter or glass. Place on ungreased baking sheet and bake in preheated 375 F. oven for about 12 minutes.

HEROS

Saturday's hero to some may be Joe Namath or Louis Tiant, but the first Saturday's hero was undoubtedly John Montagu, the Earl of Sandwich. According to *Larousse Gastronomique*, the Earl had his food brought to him at his gambling table so that he would not have to interrupt his gambling. The food was served between two slices of bread to make it easier to handle, and thus the sandwich was invented.

Gambling, picnicking or spending Sunday afternoon in front of the tube are all sandwichable occasions. Possibilities for variety are endless, but somehow most of us find ourselves in a rut when making or ordering sandwiches: ham and cheese, roast beef, tuna-fish and the ubiquitous hamburger. I hope the recipes that follow will stir your imagination, stimulate your own creative powers and give everybody a heroic meal.

JODY'S HOT SAUSAGE PAUSE

My brother Jody is an avid baseball fan. He calls his favorite sandwich a "pause" because that's the only time during the game he'll get up to prepare his specialty.

> 2 Italian sausages
> 1 small green pepper, seeded and sliced
> 1 small onion, sliced
> 2 tablespoons olive oil
> pinch oregano
> French roll
> 3 slices mozzarella cheese
> 2 strips crisp cooked bacon

Cut sausages in half and fry them until browned on each side. Remove from skillet and add green pepper, onion and oil. Stir and cook until softened. Sprinkle with oregano and place over sausage on French roll, which has been cut in half. Place slices of mozzarella cheese over sandwich and put under broiler until cheese melts. Top with bacon strips.

> *Serves 1.*

A HERO'S HERO

> 1 sesame seed bread roll
> 2 slices prosciutto
> 2 slices mortadella
> 2 slices provolone
> 2 marinated red peppers
> 2 crisp lettuce leaves
> 2 slices of tomato
> oil and vinegar

Break open roll and pull out loose bread in roll. Arrange layers of prosciutto, mortadella, provolone, red peppers, lettuce and tomato slices on bottom half of roll. Sprinkle with oil and vinegar.

> *Serves 1.*

JUICY HAMBURGER HEROS

¾ pound ground beef
1 teaspoon Worcestershire sauce
salt and pepper to taste
¼ cup chili sauce
½ cup tomato sauce
½ teaspoon dried oregano
½ teaspoon wine vinegar
2 thin slices red onion, separated into rings
¼ cup grated Cheddar cheese

Mix Worcestershire sauce, salt and pepper with hamburger. Divide mixture into two pieces. Between hands, press into 2 rectangular shapes about ¾ inch thick. Broil to desired doneness. Meanwhile, heat combined chili sauce, tomato sauce, oregano and vinegar. Place each broiled hamburger on a hero roll that has been split open and toasted.

Spoon sauce over meat and top with onion rings and cheese. Place under broiler on baking sheet until cheese melts.

Serves 2.

AND OTHER SANDWICHES

DAGWOOD SANDWICH

2 tablespoons mayonnaise
2 slices rye bread
2 slices salami
2 slices Swiss cheese
2 slices ham
2 slices tomato
1 thin slice raw onion
2 slices roast beef
1 leaf of crisp lettuce

Spread mayonnaise generously over slices of rye bread. Cover one slice with remaining ingredients and top with other slice of bread.

Serves 1 hungry man.

Make up your own Dagwood sandwich and write recipe in space provided.

_____'S DAGWOOD SANDWICH

DANISH-STYLE SANDWICHES

Danish sandwiches are traditionally served open-faced, that is, on one slice of bread. They are attractive and hearty at the same time. Each recipe below is for one sandwich.

Place a leaf of Boston lettuce on a slice of buttered black bread. Top with tiny canned Danish shrimp and a wedge of lemon. Serve with mayonnaise or mustard.

Slice liver pate on toasted rye bread. Top with mushrooms sauteed in butter and garnish with a strip of crisp bacon.

Butter a slice of whole wheat bread and cover with plenty of roast beef and garnish with sliced gherkins. Serve with mustard or mayonnaise.

Spread mustard on a slice of pumpernickel bread and top with thin slices of salami and onion rings and pimento strips.

Lightly butter a slice of white toast, then spread mustard over it. Arrange skinned and boned sardines over toast and top with thin slices of tomato, freshly chopped parsley and minced scallions.

OLD-FASHIONED HAM SALAD SANDWICH

The ham salad sandwiches of my childhood lunches bring back happy memories. They were a sublime change from the usual bologna and mustard or peanut butter and jelly. One boy in a grade school class always checked out my lunch and when a ham salad sandwich was included, he wanted a bite. Sharing it was painful, but I liked Dougy and he'd generously trade a homemade cookie for a bite of ham salad. So, here's to Dougy and school days.

> *2 cups chopped ham*
> *⅓ cup minced celery*
> *⅓ cup chopped sweet pickle*
> *1 tablespoon minced onion*
> *½ cup mayonnaise*
> *½ teaspoon prepared mustard*
> *salt and pepper to taste*

Combine ingredients and serve on buttered white toast or rye bread.

> *Makes 4 to 6 sandwiches.*

REUBEN SANDWICH

> *8 slices seeded rye bread*
> *½ cup Russian Dressing*
> *1 pound corned beef*
> *1½ cups sauerkraut*
> *8 slices ripe tomato*
> *4 slices Muenster cheese*

Each sandwich is prepared as follows: Spead two slices of bread with Russian dressing. On one slice of bread arrange layers of corned beef, sauerkraut, 2 tomato slices and one slice of cheese. Top with the other slice of bread. Wrap each sandwich in foil and place on rack in oven, which has been preheated at 375 F. Bake for 15 minutes. Remove from foil and serve immediately.

Accompany with French fried potatoes or potato chips, pickles and cold beer.

> *Serves 4.*

SALMON SALAD SANDWICH

1½ cups canned salmon, skin and bones removed
¾ cup minced celery
1 tablespoon grated onion
1 tablespoon capers
1 teaspoon lemon juice
½ cup mayonnaise
salt and freshly ground pepper to taste

Combine ingredients. Serve on black bread or white toast.

Makes 4 sandwiches.

SUBMARINE SANDWICH

Depending on what region of the country you're from you may
recognize this delectable sandwich as a submarine, grinder, hero
or hoagie. I first experienced mine as a submarine from Mike's
Submarine Shop in Albany, New York. Every time I know friends
will be in Albany, I try to talk them into bringing me one of
Mike's creations. They are fabulous; here's my favorite.

1 8-inch hero roll, cut in half. A little bread from each
    side of roll should be pulled out so ingredients will
    be easily held inside. (Roll should not be hard or it
    will be impossible to bite into.)
vinegar and oil
1 small onion, sliced thin, soaked in cold water to cover
    for 15 minutes, and dried
½ cup shredded lettuce
4 slices boiled ham
2 slices Muenster cheese
4 slices hard salami
1 tomato, sliced thin
salt and pepper

Sprinkle each side of roll generously with vinegar and oil. Arrange
onion slices and lettuce across one side of roll and top with ham,
cheese, salami and tomato slices. Season with salt and pepper and
cover with top of roll.

Serves 1 or 2.

TUNAFISH SALAD SANDWICH SPREAD

2 7-ounce cans white meat tuna
½ cup finely chopped fennel or celery
1 tablespoon minced onion
1 hard-boiled egg, chopped
1 pimento, chopped
½ teaspoon lemon juice
½ cup mayonnaise
salt and freshly ground pepper to taste

Combine ingredients. Serve on buttered rye or wholewheat bread with sliced tomato.

Makes 4 giant-size sandwiches.

TURKEY AND CRANBERRY SAUCE SANDWICH

After you've mastered the turkey there's the question of how to use what's left over. Since turkey and cranberry sauce go so well together, I did some experimenting and am pleased with the result.

4 bread rolls
butter or mayonnaise
8 slices cooked turkey
salt and freshly ground pepper to taste
4 helpings cranberry sauce
4 slices American cheese
4 lettuce leaves

Split open rolls with knife and spread each side of the inside of the rolls generously with mayonnaise or butter. Then top each bottom half of roll with 2 slices of turkey, salt and pepper, 1 layer of cranberry sauce, 1 slice of cheese and a lettuce leaf. Cover with top of roll.

Serves 4.

Serve with an ice cold beer and enjoy the game.

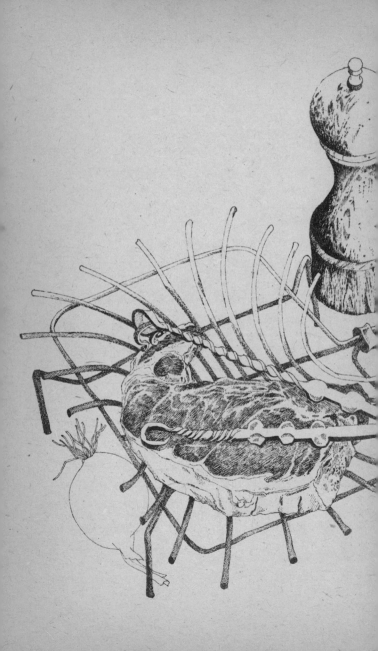

chapter 10. grilling barbecuing roasting

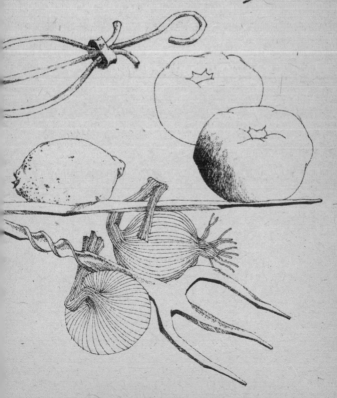

GRILLING

GRILLED FISH:

Butter, margarine or oil is required to prevent fish from drying out during cooking, since fish has a low fat content. Don't overcook fish and turn only once during cooking time. Fish is done when it is opaque and flakes easily.

GRILLED FRESH TROUT

4 fresh trout
oil
salt and pepper

Brush each trout with butter, margarine or oil. Place in well-oiled broiler basket. Grill over hot coals for 5 minutes. Brush with oil, turn and cook 5 minutes more. Salt and pepper to taste.

Serves 4.

BROILED ROCK LOBSTER TAILS

4 large rock lobster tails, thawed
¼ cup melted butter
1 tablespoon lemon juice
paprika

Cut off membrane with shears. Bend tails back and crack shell to prevent curling, or insert small skewer between shell ends and meat. Brush meat side with combined butter and lemon juice. Sprinkle with paprika. Broil shell side first for about 5 minutes. Turn, brush with sauce and cook 4 to 5 minutes. Serve immediately.

Serves 4.

MARINATED GRILLED PORK CHOPS

8 pork chops, 1-inch thick
½ teaspoon dried oregano
½ teaspoon dried thyme
1 bay leaf, crumbled
1 teaspoon salt
freshly ground pepper to taste
1 clove garlic, crushed
2 tablespoons lemon juice
4 tablespoons vegetable oil

In bowl mix herbs and seasonings, garlic, lemon juice and oil. Rub mixture into both sides of pork chop, cover and refrigerate for 6 hours, minimum. Turn chops several times while marinating. Pat chops dry with paper towels. Grill under broiler or on barbecue grill until browned on each side, about 8 minutes, but don't overcook.

Serves 4 to 6.

BEEF KEBABS ORIENTAL

2 pounds beef sirloin, cut into 2-inch cubes

MARINADE:
1 cup soy sauce
3 tablespoons oil
1 teaspoon ginger
2 cloves garlic, crushed
3 tablespoons honey
1 teaspoon prepared mustard

Combine marinade ingredients in glass bowl. Add beef cubes and stir until well coated. Cover and refrigerate for 6 hours. Place meat on skewers and grill for 8 to 12 minutes, turning once. Brush with marinade when cooked.

Serves 4.

SHISH KEBABS

2 pounds lamb, cut into 2-inch cubes

MARINADE:
½ cup olive or vegetable oil
3 tablespoons lemon juice
2 large garlic cloves, crushed
3 scallions, chopped
½ teaspoon dried oregano
1 tablespoon freshly chopped parsley
½ teaspoon salt
½ teaspoon freshly ground pepper to taste

Combine marinade in glass or ceramic bowl. Add lamb and marinate at least 6 hours in refrigerator. Fit lamb on 4 12- to 14-inch skewers and place over roasting pan that allows end of skewers to rest on sides of pan easily. Broil 3 or 4 inches from heat until meat is browned. Turn skewers to brown evenly and brush with marinade as meat cooks. Kebabs can be grilled over charcoal. Serve with hot fluffy rice.

Serves 4.

BARBECUING

BARBECUE NOTES:

Trim edge of fat so fat won't smolder too much while cooking.

Score edges of steaks or chops so they won't curl, or use a broiler basket.

Turn meat with tongs or spatula. If meat is pierced precious juices are lost.

Turn meat only once. Second side will require less cooking time.

Rub a little fat over grill or basket to prevent meat from sticking.

When coals have gray film over top, the barbecue is ready.

Place meat that is to be cooked rare on grill last.

Always season meat *after* cooking, unless using a marinade, or sauce.

HAMBURGERS:

Whether you are cooking plain hamburgers or your special stuffed burgers, the same cooking time is required. Grill 6 to 8 minutes, turn and grill 4 to 5 minutes or until desired doneness.

FRANKFURTERS:

Score frankfurters before cooking and watch carefully because they will cook very fast.

DR. BRUCE McCLENNAN'S
MARINATED BARBECUED
LEG OF LAMB

Bruce McClennan is Associate Professor of Radiology at Washington University in St. Louis, Missouri. Bruce recalls: "Back in 1967, in revolt from the hospital cafeteria scene, my colleagues and I challenged each other on weekend barbecues. My Marinated Barbecued Leg of Lamb achieved immediate acclaim. It's fast, the precision of the proportions is not critical and the opportunity to one-up the butcher's skill with a boning knife shouldn't be missed. This is one time I can guarantee that the whole operation will be a success."

5- to 6-pound leg of lamb

MARINADE:
1 cup vegetable oil
1 cup red wine
3 tablespoons red wine vinegar
2 tablespoons soy sauce
1 teaspoon rosemary
1 clove garlic, crushed
½ teaspoon salt
freshly ground pepper to taste

Debone and butterfly leg of lamb, or have butcher do it for you. This process is really very simple. Cut along the leg lengthwise through to the bone. Remove tendons as you go. Peel the meat back, stripping the bone clean. You will be left with a large flat piece of meat with fat on one side. Do not trim off fat since it will burn off on the grill. The meat will need to be flattened in spots. Achieve this by making shallow incisions in thick parts and lightly pound with tenderizer mallet. Meat should be fairly uniform in thickness.

Place meat in large shallow roasting dish. Mix marinade in bowl and pour over meat, cover and refrigerate for 4 to 6 hours (overnight if possible), and turn occasionally.

To cook, place meat fat-side-down on double thickness of heavy-duty aluminum foil over hot coals. Use kettle-top grill or make hood out of foil for grill. Turn after 15 minutes. Cooking time is about 25 minutes for a good pink-colored center. If you like it more well done, cook a little longer.

Serve with baked potatoes and mixed salad.

Serves 4 to 6.

BARBECUED SPARERIBS

4 pounds spareribs
1 bottle prepared barbecue sauce or

HOMEMADE SAUCE:
1½ cups ketchup
2 tablespoons vegetable oil
1 tablespoon Worcestershire sauce
2 dashes Tabasco sauce
¼ cup wine vinegar
½ cup beef broth
1 medium onion, finely chopped
¼ cup brown sugar

Combine sauce in pan and cook for 25 minutes.

Cook ribs over coals for 20 minutes, turning once. Brush liberally with sauce and cook until ribs are done and crispy.

Serves 4.

ROASTING

CHRIS PAPPAS' WHOLE ROAST LAMB

Chris, a native of Greece, came to the United States when he was nine years old. He credits his interest in food to his mother's good Greek cooking. He lives in Ridgewood, New Jersey, and works in Research and Development for Nabisco, Inc.

"The roasting of a lamb," says Chris, "is a traditional way for Greeks to celebrate holidays and festive occasions. I have many pleasant memories of my family's trips to Nashua, New Hampshire, a city heavily populated by Greeks, to celebrate Easter with my relatives. At such gatherings we danced to bouzouki music, savored the delicious traditional foods and had our appetites whetted by the marvelous aroma as we took our turns rotating the lamb.

"I've recently roasted lambs for our neighborhood block party and for the christening of my daughter, Michele Lynn. It's quite a conversation piece and seems to draw people together. Roasting the lamb is a rather Herculean task which is usually performed by the men of one or more Greek families. I'd advise anyone trying it to find a Greek friend who has done one before and who will not only share his knowledge, but also his equipment."

> 1 whole cleaned spring lamb, 25 to 35 pounds

> SEASONING:
> Mix together in a bowl:
> 1 cup salt
> 1 tablespoon white pepper
> ½ cup oregano
> ¼ teaspoon garlic powder

EQUIPMENT:
1 large spit: approximately 6 feet long, pointed iron or wooden rod for holding meat over the fire. The diameter can range from ½ inch to 1½ inches. It should have a turning handle at one end.
2 stakes: Y-shaped to hold spit.
Butcher cord: To tie lamb to spit.

Needle and heavy thread: For sewing up cavity.

Sharp pointed knife and butcher's cleaver.

Meat holders: Metal prongs to secure lamb to spit (optional).

Several bags charcoal: About 20 pounds, depending upon weather conditions and size of lamb.

Preparation of Pit: Prepare a barbecue pit slightly larger than the length of the lamb. Line bottom of pit with flat stones, a sheet of metal or heavy foil. Drive stakes into ground at each end of the pit (slightly off center). Prepare a good charcoal fire.

Preparation of Lamb: Insert spit through the lamb. Secure centered lamb onto spit by making holes on both sides of spine in 3 places: before kidney chops or hind legs, middle of rib cage and at the end of shoulder blades. Put string through holes and tie tightly to prevent slipping during cooking. Flatten front legs to neck and tie securely. Spread and extend hind legs before tying.

Season shoulder blades by making two slashes the width of a knife and putting some seasoning inside slashes. Plug slashes with fat which has been cut from inside of lamb. Repeat for hind quarters. Season inside of lamb with the remaining seasoning, using some to rub the outer skin surface. Using a large needle and heavy thread sew up entire belly and rib cage of lamb.

Place spit onto Y-shaped stakes approximately 1 to 1½ feet from coals. During the first hour, the coals are spread evenly the full length of lamb. Turn lamb continuously about 40 rpm. As lamb cooks, rake coals away from the center of the lamb and concentrate the heat on the shoulder and rump sections. Depending on weather conditions, heat reflectors may be used to concentrate heat on critical areas. Turning may be slowed as cooking continues. Cooking time varies due to conditions. A 30-pound lamb will cook in about 4 hours. Check for doneness when meat starts separating from shoulder blades and legs. Lamb is cooked if hip bone exposes itself and is cool to the touch. Remove cooked lamb still on spit and lean against a wall for 15 minutes to cool.

Carve with meat cleaver and sharp knife.

Serves 45.

chapter 11· desserts

An appealing dessert at the conclusion of a meal, whether it's a gooey cream dessert or fresh fruit and cheese, is as vital to the meal's success as the perfect entree. I asked a number of men for their favorite dessert. Chocolate desserts that ranged from simple ice cream to rich mousse were highest on a long list.

Since most desserts can be made in advance of the rest of a meal, you can be as elaborate as you like. Desserts are always challenging and possibly the most rewarding dish of all. Fledgling dessert makers should find it reassuring to discover how uncomplicated making pie dough or a cake really is. Be sure to read the recipe all the way through and follow directions closely and baking will soon be your favorite sport.

MARTIN RAPP'S CARROT CAKE
(With thanks to Anne Jeffreys)

Martin Rapp, Director of Publications of the Modern Art Museum, strives for gastronomical excellence. He demonstrated his culinary skills at a fabulous Saturday night dinner party that I attended by cooking and serving the entire meal. His wife, Samantha, set the table and removed the dishes, course by course. They cleaned up together. It's a regular and very successful routine.

Martin's Carrot Cake is pure gold. He says he hates the idea of carrot cake, but this one is just so good he can't resist it. Toasted and served with butter, this cake is hard to stop eating.

> 3 eggs
> 2 cups sugar
> 2 cups grated carrots
> 1½ cups vegetable oil
> 1 cup crushed pineapple with juice
> 1 cup angel flake coconut
> 2¼ cups flour
> 2 teaspoons cinnamon
> 1 teaspoon baking soda
> 1 teaspoon salt
> 1 teaspoon vanilla
> 1 cup walnuts
> ½ cup white raisins, optional

Beat eggs lightly. Add sugar and beat until lemon yellow. Add carrots and mix. Add oil, pineapple and coconut and combine. Add remaining ingredients and mix well. Fill two greased loaf pans about half full and bake in preheated 350 F. oven for about 1 hour. Remove from oven and let cakes rest half an hour before turning out.

COCONUT ORANGE CAKE

Many men I know love cake but would never think of baking one themselves. It seems too great a task. Well, here's a cake that is truly easy to bake. Just read the directions and you'll see.

> 1 package yellow cake mix
> 4 eggs
> ½ cup vegetable oil
> 1 package instant coconut pudding
> 1 cup orange juice

Combine ingredients well in a large bowl. You'll have to beat mixture about 5 minutes with a large wooden spoon. Grease a 10-inch tube pan and pour batter into it. Place in preheated 350 F. oven and bake for about 40 minutes. Test for doneness by sticking a wooden toothpick into cake. If it comes out clean, the cake is done. Allow cake to cool 10 minutes before taking it out of pan. Eat plain or serve with your favorite ice cream.

MOUSSE CHOCOLATE CAKE WITH EVA'S CHOCOLATE FROSTING

> 2 cups milk
> 1½ cups granulated sugar
> 8 ounces butter, or 2 sticks
> 8 ounces unsweetened chocolate, cut into small pieces
> 4 eggs, separated
> 2½ cups all-purpose flour
> 2 teaspoons baking powder
> ⅛ teaspoon salt

Heat milk, sugar, butter and chocolate in saucepan until butter and chocolate have melted, stirring constantly. Remove pan from heat and allow mixture to cool. Beat in egg yolks. Add flour, baking powder and salt and mix for about 5 minutes. Beat egg whites until stiff and fold into mixture. Butter 9 by 9-inch cake pan and pour batter into pan. Place in pan of hot water that comes halfway up side of cake pan. Bake in preheated 375 F. oven for 1 hour. Cool and frost.

EVA'S CHOCOLATE FROSTING

1 can sweetened condensed milk
1 tablespoon water
pinch salt
2 squares unsweetened chocolate
½ teaspoon vanilla

In top pan of a double boiler, blend all ingredients except for vanilla. Stir until thickened and remove from heat. Add vanilla and combine. Cool. Spread over cake with cake spatula.

BLUEBERRY CAKE WITH CINNAMON CRUMB TOPPING

1 pint blueberries
2½ cups flour
¼ cup brown sugar
1 cup granulated sugar
1 teaspoon cinnamon
1 stick butter (8 tablespoons)
2 teaspoons baking powder
½ teaspoon salt
1 egg, lightly beaten
1 teaspoon vanilla
½ cup milk

Wash blueberries and remove any stems, drain and dry on paper towels. In small bowl place ¼ cup flour, the brown sugar, ¼ cup granulated sugar and the cinnamon. Add ½ stick of butter (or 4 tablespoons) and cut mixture with knife until crumb-like. Into a large bowl put the remaining flour and sugar, the baking powder, salt, egg, vanilla and milk. Gently fold in blueberries and turn into buttered 9 by 9-inch square baking pan. Sprinkle crumb-cinnamon mixture on top and bake in preheated 375 F. oven for 45 to 50 minutes. Cool at least 15 minutes before serving.

Yield: 9 servings.

BOB DAVIS' APPLE CAKE

Helen and Bob Davis bought a handsome Victorian house in East Haddam, Connecticut, ten years ago and turned it into their home and a complex of lovely shops called The Seraph. Lucky customers can buy anything from fashionable clothing and jewelry to china and kitchenware. Lucky friends, welcome to stop by for a visit, usually gather in the sunny second-floor modern kitchen.

Bob, an interior designer, has worked his wizardry on the whole house, but the kitchen is my favorite room. Four tall windows with western, southern and eastern exposure accentuate the large black and yellow kitchen. A long rectangular marble table with black leather and chrome chairs is situated at one end of the room by the windows. There you can sit and admire the Connecticut countryside or the kitchen's professional range, abundant cabinet space, a butcher-block-covered center island with storage space and a warming drawer below and 2-tiered hanging glass shelves overhead, the wall-attached 48-unit beehive spice rack, a healthy ficus tree or the Spanish-tiled floor. And, of course, a large refrigerator-freezer and dish washer. A dream kitchen.

Bob is the rare man who enjoys food shopping. He's as discriminating in the market as he is in his designing, especially when shopping for the ingredients for his Apple Cake for one of the Davis' "Dessert Evenings." Guests arrive after 9 p.m. and are served a variety of desserts (always Bob's Apple Cake), coffee and brandy. If it's a chilly evening, he also prepares a crackling fire.

> ⅓ cup Calvados (Applejack or rum may be substituted)
> 1 cup currants
> 2 cups flour
> ¼ teaspoon salt

> 2 teaspoons baking soda
> 1 teaspoon nutmeg
> 1 teaspoon cinnamon
> ½ teaspoon allspice
> ½ cup sweet butter
> 1 cup brown sugar
> 2 eggs
> ¾ cup coarsely chopped walnuts
> 2 cups applesauce

Preheat oven to 350 F. Butter a large loaf pan (12 x 4 x 3 inches). In a small bowl combine Calvados and currants. In a medium-size bowl combine sifted flour, salt, baking soda, nutmeg, cinnamon and allspice. Set aside. In a large bowl cream butter, sugar and eggs together until light in color and smooth. Add currants and liquor to butter mixture with nuts and applesauce. Mix well. Add a quarter of flour mixture to ingredients in large bowl and combine. Continue adding a quarter of flour mixture to large bowl and combining well each time until all ingredients are mixed. Pour into buttered pan and bake for 1 hour or until done.

EVA LOWE'S POUND CAKE

Everything we ate at my grandparents' farm in North Texas was either grown or raised on their land. Each summer I spent there in my childhood, I had chores of collecting eggs and churning butter. My occasional reward was one of my grandmother's memorable pound cakes.

> 1 cup sugar
> ½ pound lightly salted butter, at room temperature
> 5 whole eggs
> 2 cups flour
> 1 ½ teaspoons vanilla

Cream sugar and butter together until very light and fluffy. Beat in 1 egg at a time. Gradually add flour, beating until smooth, and then add vanilla and beat. Turn into greased loaf pan and bake in preheated 350 F. oven for about 1 hour. Let cake rest 1 hour before cutting. Cake flavor improves with time.

ITALIAN CHEESECAKE

3 pounds ricotta cheese
2 cups granulated sugar
1 pint heavy cream
4 eggs
3 egg yolks
½ teaspoon vanilla
½ teaspoon almond extract

Combine all ingredients in large bowl. Puree mixture, a few cupfuls at a time, in blender. Pour into well-greased 10-inch round spring-form cake pan. Bake in preheated 400 F. oven on baking sheet for 1 hour and 15 minutes. Cool for an hour or so at room temperature. Refrigerate for several hours or overnight. Remove sides of spring-form pan.

Serves 12 to 14.

JACK ABBOTT'S ORANGE KISS CAKE

This unusually moist cake is a favorite of Jack and Helen Abbott. They live on Mallorca and often serve this delicious cake for tea with English friends.

1 large orange
1 cup raisins
½ cup finely chopped walnuts
2 cups sifted flour
1 cup sugar
1 teaspoon baking soda
1 teaspoon salt
½ cup vegetable oil
1 cup milk
2 eggs

TOPPING:
⅓ cup sugar
1 teaspoon cinnamon
¼ cup walnuts, finely chopped

Squeeze juice from orange and reserve for topping. Grate rind of
orange and add to raisins and walnuts. Set aside. In large mixing
bowl combine flour, sugar, soda and salt. Add oil and ¾ cup
milk. Beat at low speed for 1½ minutes. Add eggs and remaining
¼ cup milk. Beat 1½ minutes more. Fold in raisin-nut mixture.
Turn into greased and floured 12- by 8-inch baking pan. Place in
preheated 350 F. oven for about 45 minutes or until cake is done.
Drip orange juice over warm cake. Sprinkle with mixture of ⅓ cup
sugar, 1 teaspoon cinnamon and ¼ cup walnuts. Let rest for 1
hour before cutting.

MARTIN POLLNER'S QUEEN OF PUDDING

*Martin Pollner, formerly Deputy Assistant Secretary of the United
States Treasury Department, is a trial attorney in New York City.
Brooklyn born, Martin's fondest food memory is his mother's dinner of
chicken fricassee and potato pancakes followed by Oreos and milk. His
now sophisticated palate prompts him to cook when he craves a special
dish. Regretfully, he seldom cooks his Queen of Pudding dessert, because he claims he'd rather endure a two-month grueling trial than separate the eggs and beat the whites for the meringue. He is contemplat-
ing my suggestion of using an egg separator and an electric mixer.*

> 1 cup milk
> 2 tablespoons butter
> 1½ cups dried bread crumbs
> ⅔ cup sugar
> grated rind of 1 lemon
> 2 egg yolks (save whites for meringue)
> ¼ cup raspberry jam
>
> MERINGUE:
> 2 egg whites
> ½ cup confectioners' sugar
> pinch of salt

Bring milk just to the boil and remove from heat immediately. Stir
in butter, bread crumbs, sugar and lemon rind. Cool for a few
moments before adding beaten egg yolks. Turn mixture into buttered Pyrex loaf pan. Place in preheated 350 F. oven and cook for

25 minutes. Remove from oven and spread raspberry jam over top of pudding. Prepare meringue by whipping egg whites until fluffy. Add confectioners' sugar and pinch of salt and beat until stiff, about 5 minutes with electric mixer. Spread meringue over raspberry jam and place in low oven for 2 hours.

Serves 4.

CHRISTMAS NUT CAKE

¾ pound butter or margarine (3 sticks)
2 cups sugar
6 eggs, separated
4 cups flour
4 teaspoons cinnamon
½ teaspoon allspice
½ cup molasses
1 teaspoon soda powder
1½ pounds raisins
7 cups pecans or walnuts
½ cup red wine

Cream butter and sugar together. Beat egg yolks and stir in. Add half of flour and all of cinnamon and allspice to mixture and combine. Mix molasses and soda powder in small bowl and add to cake mixture along with rest of flour. Beat egg whites until stiff and fold into batter. Finally, add raisins, nuts and red wine. Fold into mixture and pour into 2 well-greased loaf pans. Bake in preheated 325 F. oven for about 1½ hours. Test for doneness by inserting thin sharp knife into cake. If it comes out clean cake is done.

PIE DOUGH

1¼ cups all-purpose flour
¼ teaspoon salt
¼ teaspoon sugar*
1 stick sweet butter
3 tablespoons ice-cold water

* Omit sugar in recipes which aren't desserts such as meat pies.

Sift together flour and salt. Add sugar and place on marble, board or formica surface. Cut butter into flour mixture until it has crumb consistency. Add water in center and knead until smooth. Refrigerate, if a hot day, for 30 minutes, covered in bowl. Lightly flour board or other surface and roll out pie dough with rolling pin, which should also be lightly floured, until dough is about ⅛ inch thick. Roll dough over rolling pin and turn over on to pie plate or tart pan. Trim off extra dough and shape edges. Fill and bake according to directions for particular pie recipe, or bake pie dough blind. To do this fill dough with 1 cup dried navy beans, and place in preheated 400 F. oven for 8 to 10 minutes until crust is lightly browned. Remove beans, and save for next pie baked blind.

Yield: 1 9- to 10-inch pie crust.

PECAN OR WALNUT PIE

3 eggs, lightly beaten
1 cup dark corn syrup
3 tablespoons melted butter
½ teaspoon cinnamon
½ teaspoon nutmeg
¼ teaspoon salt
1 teaspoon vanilla
1½ cups chopped pecans or walnuts
1 9-inch unbaked pie shell

Mix together eggs, corn syrup, butter, cinnamon, nutmeg, salt, vanilla and nuts. Pour mixture into pie shell and bake in preheated 375 F. oven for 40 minutes until crust is golden.

Serve with ice cream or whipped cream.

BILL MURFIN'S PEANUT BUTTER PIE

"I first tasted this pie in Dogpatch, Arkansas, but it tastes even better on a sailboat off Long Island and on a mountainside in the Virgin Islands," says Bill Murfin, Regional Director of the Small Business Administration in New Orleans.

> 3 cups milk
> ½ cup sugar
> ¼ teaspoon salt
> 3 heaping tablespoons cornstarch
> 3 egg yolks, beaten
> 2 tablespoons butter
> 1 teaspoon vanilla
> ½ cup peanut butter, chunky or smooth

Heat milk in saucepan. Meanwhile, mix sugar, salt, cornstarch and egg yolks together. Add to milk and cook until thickened, always stirring. Add butter, vanilla and peanut butter. When well combined pour into graham-cracker pie shell.

AUDREY ROOS' COGNAC PIE

> 5 egg yolks
> ¾ cup sugar
> 1 envelope unflavored gelatin
> ¼ cup cold water
> ¼ cup cognac
> 1 cup heavy cream
> 1 9-inch graham-cracker crust

Beat egg yolks until thick and lemon colored. Slowly beat in sugar. Soften gelatin in water and add cognac. Heat in pan over boiling water until gelatin is dissolved. Add gelatin to egg mixture, stirring quickly. Whip cream and fold into mixture. Pour into pie shell and chill until firm.

Decorate with shaved chocolate, if desired.

CHOCOLATE SOUFFLÉ

I hope I can convince you that a soufflé is not a thing to fear. Follow directions carefully and the result will be heavenly: light, rich and spectacular.

> 4 tablespoons butter
> 4 tablespoons flour
> 1½ cups milk, heated
> 6 egg yolks
> granulated sugar
> 6 ounces unsweetened chocolate
> 9 egg whites

In saucepan melt butter and add flour. Stir with whisk over medium low heat for 1 minute. Slowly pour in hot milk, constantly stirring, until sauce is smooth and thickened. Remove from heat to cool. Beat together egg yolks and ⅔ cup sugar until lemon colored. Pour into sauce, stirring. In top of double boiler with boiling water in lower pan, melt chocolate with 2 tablespoons sugar. Cool slightly and stir into sauce, then combine. Fit a piece of foil (making a collar) around a 2½-quart soufflé dish and secure with string. Butter soufflé dish and foil. Place 2 tablespoons sugar in dish and tilt until buttered surface is covered. Beat egg whites until stiff and fold into sauce in large bowl. Pour soufflé mixture into prepared soufflé dish and bake in preheated 350 F. oven for 45 minutes. Remove foil collar and serve at once.

> Serves 6 to 8.

RUM FUDGE BALLS

> 2 cups finely crushed vanilla wafers
> ⅓ cup rum
> 12 ounces semi-sweet chocolate morsels
> ¾ cup sweetened condensed milk
> sweetened cocoa

Combine vanilla wafer crumbs and rum. Melt chocolate in top of double boiler. Stir in sweetened condensed milk. Pour over crumb mixture and shape into 1-inch balls. Roll in cocoa. Store in closed container in refrigerator.

FRESH FRUIT AND YOGHURT COMPOTE

(all fruit should be thoroughly chilled)
1 cantaloupe, peeled and seeded and cut into bite-size
   pieces
1 Delicious apple, cored and diced
1 cup sliced strawberries
1 banana, sliced
2 peaches, peeled, pitted and sliced
1 cup blueberries
½ pint plain yoghurt
¼ cup brown sugar

Place fruit in large bowl. Add yoghurt and brown sugar. Gently
toss.

Serves 4.

WHOLE PEACHES IN RASPBERRY
WINE SAUCE

2 quarts water
8 fresh ripe peaches
1 10-ounce package frozen raspberries
¼ cup red currant jam
1 cup red wine
¼ cup sugar
½ pint heavy cream

Bring water to a boil in a large saucepan. Gently lower peaches
into water, cover, and leave for about 4 minutes. Remove with
slotted spoon and drain. Peel peaches and leave whole. Cool.
Place two peaches in each individual dessert plate. Combine raspberries, red currant jam, wine and sugar, bring to a boil and reduce heat to a simmer, stirring. Cook for about 5 minutes, stirring, until sauce thickens slightly. Spoon sauce over peaches and
serve with heavy cream—and extra sugar, if desired.

Serves 4.

AMBROSIA GREBANIER

This is Bernard Grebanier's delicious variant on an old Southern dessert.

> 2 cups shredded coconut
> 2 cups mandarin oranges
> 2 cups grapefruit sections
> 2 cups kumquats
> granulated sugar
> sherry wine

In a glass jar—large enough for the quantity being made, but one which will fit into a refrigerator—make layers of coconut shreds, oranges, grapefruit and kumquats. Cover with a tablespoon of sugar or two. If canned fruit is used, the syrup may be substituted for the sugar. Pour two tablespoons of sherry over the fruit. Repeat these layers until ingredients are used, always in the same order.

Serves 8

FRESH STRAWBERRIES WITH CRÈME FRAÎCHE

2 pints fresh strawberries, stems removed

CRÈME FRAÎCHE:
1 cup heavy cream
1 tablespoon buttermilk

Place heavy cream in glass bowl or jar and add buttermilk. Stir and let stand at room temperature for 8 to 32 hours until cream has thickened. Bowl or jar should be slightly covered. Store cream in refrigerator or use immediately.

Prepare Crème Fraîche and spoon generously on fresh strawberries.

Serves 6.

Chapter 12. Parties

COCKTAILS FOR 24

Entertaining at home often seems unnecessarily complicated to men, whether it's a cocktail party, informal meal or special dinner party. All three should be joyful occasions and only a few simple preparations are required for everyone to have a good time, including the host. A friend has offered to share his basic formula for cocktail parties. Everything he serves is put together in advance. These preparations he does himself. Here is his recipe for a cocktail party for 24.

BAR:

3 bottles scotch
1 bottle dry vermouth
2 bottles vodka
2 bottles gin
1 bottle bourbon
2 gallon jugs dry white wine
6 quarts soda
6 quarts tonic
cocktail olives and onions
lemon and lime peels
large bag of ice
24 tall glasses ⎫
24 cocktail glasses ⎭ glass or plastic
cocktail napkins

FOOD:

2 pounds sliced boiled ham, cut slices in half and fold in half, arrange on large platter in rows
2 pounds sliced roast beef, slices cut in half and folded in half, arrange on platter with ham in rows
2 pounds Genoa salami, arranged on platter
2 pounds sliced Swiss cheese, each slice cut into 3 pieces and arranged on platter with salami
(Garnish each platter with bunches of parsley or watercress)

Salad Bowl filled with mixture of black olives (2 16-ounce cans jumbo size), 1 large head of raw cauliflower, cut into small flowerets, and 2 pints cherry tomatoes, cleaned and stems removed.

2 packages of party rye and 2 packages of party pumpernickel bread arranged on napkin in bread basket.

Small bowl of herb mayonnaise with spoon
Small bowl of mustard with spoon
Butter in dish with knife
Salt and peppermill
Bowl of mixed nuts
Large bowl of popcorn
Platter of mixed cookies
Bowl of chocolate covered mints

24 plates, china or paper
24 forks, stainless or silver
24 dinner napkins, cloth or paper (have extras handy)

Flowers

GOURMET DINNER PARTY MENUS

STEVE SOHMER'S GRANDE BOUFFE

Steve Sohmer is a film maker and president of the Steve Sohmer, Inc., a multi-media promotion firm.

"My mother spoiled me," Steve declares. "I grew up in a home where coq au vin and canard l'orange were regular dinner-time events. Even on Rosh Hashanah, we dined on carrot soufflé.

"My wife's meat loaf broke up our marriage.

"Bachelorhood was a horror. One morning, a young lady of my acquaintance set out to make soft-boiled eggs for herself and medium-boiled eggs for me—by putting on two pots of water. Since my mother would not take me back, I had to learn to cook. The qualities of a successful bachelor are the same as those that make a successful cook: prepare in advance; concentrate on a few dishes each season; save your strength for the moments of high drama.

"The menu below may be prepared in a leisurely fashion over one evening and one afternoon—except for the Bouillabaise, which must be finished, presented and devoured in a flash of passion. These dishes, like French women, have flowery names and an elegant appearance, but their essential parts are familiar, and they are easy to make."

LE DÎNER MENU	Vin
Consomme au citron, quenelles de gibier	A nutty Oloroso sherry (William & Humbert Canasta Cream)
Terrine Souzeraine	
	A spicy white (Kitterle Traminer Schlumberger '71)
Bouillabaisse Américaine	
	A full, rounded white (Clos des Mouches '71)
Pouding de Riz Sauvage	
	Champagne
Café Diable	

Recipes

CONSOMME AU CITRON, QUENELLES DE GIBIER

This soup is rich and delicate at the same time. It's also quick and unusual. If you're a hunter, you might want to prepare your own pate of game; otherwise, buy it tinned.

> *1 cup game pate*
> *2 egg yolks*
> *3 tablespoons butter*
> *salt*
> *cayenne pepper*
> *2 cans beef consomme (concentrated)*
> *1 cup water*
> *¾ lemon juice*

Form the game pate into 12 small quenelles (small oval-shaped pieces), dip in the egg yolk and saute briefly in butter. Sprinkle lightly with salt and cayenne pepper. Remove from heat and keep warm in covered dish.

Meanwhile, combine the concentrated consomme and water and bring to a boil. Reduce heat and add the lemon juice. Serve two quenelles in each plate of soup. Keep the servings small to emphasize the delicacy of the flavor.

Serves 6.

TERRINE SOUZERAINE

This recipe makes an unusual and dramatic presentation at the table. The rich breast of duck makes a wonderful contrast to the other meats, but it may be omitted for economy's sake.

> 1 pound chicken breasts, skinned and boned
> 1 pound veal scallops
> 1 4-pound duck (optional)
> salt
> white pepper
> 1/2 cup Madeira
> 1 pound bacon
> 1 large white onion, finely chopped
> 1/4 pound shelled, unsalted pistachio nuts
> 1/2 teaspoon dried thyme
> 1 bay leaf
> 1 cup dry white wine
> 2 cans beef consomme (concentrated)
> 1 package unflavored gelatin

To skin and bone the chicken simply pull the skin off and use a sharp thin knife to cut the meat away from the bone; but you can have the butcher do this for you. The breast meat will also need to be flattened slightly, as well as the veal. This is easily done with the use of a tenderizer mallet; or, again, the friendly butcher will do it for you. Set these aside until ready to use. Remove the breast from the duck by carefully peeling back the skin and then inserting a thin knife blade between the breast and the bone on each side. Sprinkle with salt and pepper and marinate the breast pieces in a small bowl in the Madeira.

Line a 2-quart terrine with bacon strips so that the strips come up the sides and hang out over the edge.

Spread a layer of veal in the bottom of the terrine. Then sprinkle with white pepper and spread a light layer of chopped onion. Next a layer of chicken breast, sprinkle with pistachios. Next a layer of bacon. Proceed in this sequence until the terrine is half filled.

Remove the breast of duck from the marinade and place it in the center of the terrine. Then begin the sequence of layers up to the top of the terrine. Cover with a layer of bacon and fold the strips of bacon over the top layer of bacon to seal the terrine. Sprinkle with thyme, add a bay leaf and cover with white wine.

Stand the terrine with cover on in a pan of hot water in a pre-heated 350 F. oven for 90 minutes. Remove the terrine from the oven and pour off excess fluid and fat. Cooking will "tighten up" the meat and the bloc will have pulled away from the walls of the dish.

Cover with a sheet of aluminum foil and place a heavy weight on the terrine. A brick would be ideal, but since you may not have one in your kitchen, a heavy can will do. Let stand overnight in a warm place. This is called "bricking"; it forces the excess fat and fluid out of the terrine.

In the morning, pour off the fluid and place the terrine in the re-frigerator until thoroughly chilled. Prepare an aspic by combining the consomme and gelatin in a saucepan and mixing thoroughly. Bring to a boil and remove from heat.

Pour the aspic over contents of terrine, skim off any fat that rises and return to the refrigerator.

To serve, slice off the end of the bloc and remove from the dish. Then keep slices ⅜-inch thick and lift from the dish with care.

Serve with cornichons (little gherkins) and French mustard. This terrine will yield 12 slices. It will keep in the refrigerator for a week or longer.

BOUILLABAISE AMERICAINE

The secret of this recipe is the quick poaching of the seafood, which is not placed in the stock until the dinner guests have already started on their first course.

>*½ cup chopped onion*
>*½ cup chopped celery*
>*¼ cup olive oil*
>*1 teaspoon fennel seeds*
>*1 bay leaf*
>*16 ounces bottled clam juice*
>*½ bottle dry white wine*
>*4 16-ounce cans peeled whole tomatoes*
>*2 pounds halibut, cut into 3-inch pieces*
>*24 littleneck clams*
>*24 mussels*
>*2 pounds Alaskan king crab legs*
>*1 pound sea scallops*
>*24 medium shrimp*

Saute the onion and celery in the oil with fennel and bay leaf, but do not allow to brown. Add the clam juice, wine and tomatoes. Simmer 30 minutes. Add the halibut and simmer.

Scrub the mussels and clean them. In large kettle place ½ inch of water and bring it to a boil. Add mussels and clams, cover and cook about 6 minutes until shells open. Discard any mussels which do not open. Drain. Break the crab legs into individual joints. When your guests have begun their first course, turn up a medium flame under the stock—which should be quite rich and aromatic by now, having cooked about 1 hour. Then layer the seafood in the stock. This is very important, since the shrimp cook faster than the crab legs. Follow this order: crab legs first, then scallops, then clams, then mussels, then shrimp. Make sure the stock covers all.

Cook only until the shrimp tighten and begin to redden slightly.

Serve the seafood in shallow bowls and cover with stock. Serve with crusty French bread—no vegetables, nothing else.

Serves 6.

POUDING DE RIZ SAUVAGE

This is an original recipe which emphasizes the delicate flavor of wild rice. It is not heavy, sticky or overly sweet because it is made with meringue and chilled, not baked. Wild rice is expensive, but this elegant, unusual dessert makes the most of it.

>   8 ounces wild rice
>   salt
>   6 egg yolks
>   1 cup sugar
>   1 tablespoon vanilla
>   1 quart milk
>   2 packages gelatin, unflavored
>   ½ cup water
>   8 egg whites

Parboil the rice for 20 minutes in lightly salted water to cover the rice. Drain carefully. Stir egg yolks into rice. In saucepan add sugar and vanilla to milk, bring to a boil and add to the rice. Place in preheated 350 F. oven for 45 minutes in casserole dish. Remove from oven and pour off excess milk, leaving rice moist. Rice will now be slightly undercooked and will have a light, chewy consistency. Cool. Stir in gelatin which has softened in the water. Beat egg whites until stiff and fold into rice, being careful not to break grains. Place in a decorative serving dish and place in freezer compartment until set. Do not allow to freeze. Spoon into dessert dishes, add a dash of Tia Maria liqueur and a dollop of whipped cream.

>   Serves 6 to 8.

CAFÉ DIABLE

This is a fancy coffee prepared at tableside with a gee-whiz flambé show. It has a seductive orange-liqueur flavor and a wonderful aroma derived from the flaming cloves and orange peel.

> *juice of 2 oranges*
> *peel of 2 oranges, taken off in one long strip*
> *1 cinnamon stick*
> *¼ cup sugar*
> *1 cup cointreau*
> *cloves*
> *10 cups hot coffee*
> *5 teaspoons instant espresso granules*
> *⅓ cup cognac*

Place juice of two oranges in chafing dish with one peel, cinnamon stick, sugar and ⅔ cup of cointreau. Allow to marinate for at least two hours. Remove cinnamon stick and peel. Cut the peel off from an orange in one long strip. Stick cloves into peel at 1-inch intervals. Skewer with fork at one end so that the peel hangs in a long strip. Prepare 10 cups of coffee in a pot and stir in espresso granules. Bring the chafing dish to the table and light the burner. Place the remaining cointreau, mixed with the cognac, in a large ladle. Heat the mixture so that it catches fire; it will burn with an almost invisible blue flame. Turn off lights.

Hold the orange peel so that it dangles over the chafing dish and gingerly pour the flaming mixture down the peel. The liqueur will follow the curl of the peel, lighting the cloves and creating a lively show. When the liqueur is exhausted, discard the peel and add the coffee-espresso mixture.

Ladle into small cups; it's very potent.

Serves 6—with seconds for the unwary.

DINNER PARTY HINTS

For the table

> Tablecloth or place mats, if sit-down dinner
> Flowers
> Dinner plates
> Salad plates, if sit-down dinner
> Knives, forks and spoons
> Cloth napkins
> Wine glasses
> Water goblet, if sit-down dinner
> At least two sets of salt and pepper shakers; one at
>   each end of table.
> Wine
> Bread in basket lined with napkin
> Butter in dish with knife
> Trivets for hot dishes
> You'll need dessert plates and fork or spoon, de-
>   pending on dessert.
> Coffee cups and saucers
> Creamer and sugar bowl with spoon

Perfect timing

Timing is crucial when you are serving a special meal. Poor timing
can ruin the most elegantly assembled menu. Once you have selected your menu, sit down and carefully map out the timing for
each recipe. Determine how long it will take to prepare each dish,
which may be started before guests arrive and which need last-
minute attention. If a dish needs to be chilled, that too must be
considered in the total planning, as well as other time-consuming
processes such as marinating, peeling, chopping and mixing.

The size of your stove and oven plays an important part in the
scheduling game. If you have a small oven, don't plan to serve a
roast and biscuits and a casserole—all take oven space and require
different temperatures. Four burners will not accommodate six sauce-

pans unless the dishes they hold can be heated at different times during the preparation of the meal. And check out the pans you will need. Even I have been caught with two dishes to cook and only one pan of the appropriate size. All of this pre-planning may sound fussy and obvious, but it will save having to change a menu or method at the last minute.

Desserts, such as cakes and pies, can be made before the rest of the dinner and will keep until served. Often, appetizers and soups can be prepared earlier in the day. You should have time to greet guests, help them to cocktails, and enjoy a drink and appetizer yourself before you rush off to the kitchen to finish cooking dinner.

Fish cooks quickly unless it is a large fish or long-cooking stew. Meat usually takes the longest cooking time. While it is cooking, you can cook the vegetables and prepare the salad and dressing. The side dishes—vegetables and rice or noodles or potatoes—should be placed in their proper pots and pans before the guests arrive so that all you have to do is add the hot liquid to cook. If potatoes are peeled, let them stand in cold salted water until ready to cook. (The above directions will, of course, depend upon the particular recipe for each dish.) Lettuce for a salad can be washed, drained and wrapped in cloth or paper towels and refrigerated until ready to combine with other ingredients. The dressing can be prepared ahead, but should be mixed and poured over the salad just before you toss and serve it.

Everything will be much easier if you plan your menu so that the cooking times vary. If everything takes thirty minutes you will be whirling about madly trying to get it all attractively arranged in serving dishes and still keep it hot.

There will be a different formula for each meal and no matter how experienced you become at cooking for guests or family, you will still want to plot your timing carefully in advance. A kitchen timer is an invaluable aid to help remind you when a dish needs to be uncovered, stirred, turned or is done.

COOKING FOR CHILDREN

Cooking for children is never easy. Their food preferences depend not only on what is served in their home, but also on other children's likes and dislikes, and on what is advertised on television and radio. Anecdotes about the peculiarities of children's taste and their pickiness abound. The little boy who doesn't want anything on his plate to touch (Jean Kerr carried this to the extreme with her tale of the child's tuna fish sandwich: the tuna, bread, celery and mayonnaise were all on separate plates and eaten in succession); a niece who refused an American cheese sandwich because the cheese was Borden's and not Kraft's. The child of a friend who would not drink the glass of milk until he made sure that it was his brand, seemed to me to be the absolute nadir. Shaping a child's eating habits should not be underestimated; begin early to encourage a curious and cosmopolitan palate. Another curiosity: all the men I interviewed remembered their mother's special dishes with reverence, no matter how pedestrian the dish. None of them remembered their father's special dish although some recalled that their fathers were excellent cooks. Sounds like an old taboo to me. So maybe we'll be making history by helping daddy produce winners that his children will remember with fondness.

Food for children may sometimes have to be a little theatrical, but it should always be nutritional. Invite the children to help in the kitchen. It can bring kids and their fathers closer and educate them at the same time.

KEN AULETTA'S FRIED MEATBALLS

Ken Auletta writes a column for the New York Daily News *and is a writer for the* New Yorker. *He also co-hosts a weekly* TV *interview program for public broadcasting. Ken's a good friend who once confided that one of his greatest fears is that of the pain of hunger. The glow on his face when he's hearing the dinner menu recited illustrates to me how happy food can make a man. His contribution is delicious, and as irresistible to most kids as it was to him.*

"I hate meatballs. Correction. I hate those well-done hamburgers masquerading as meatballs in most restaurants or on hero sandwiches. Tiny rocks of ground beef through which no sauce can penetrate. There

is too much meat. No egg. No bread. No cheese. No fluffiness. Try to slice them with your fork and they will splash sauce on your shirt. Try to bite into them on a hero and like marbles they will squirt out.

"There must be—and is—a better way. My meatball revelation first came to me as a little boy in Coney Island, Brooklyn. Every other Sunday the family journeyed to my grandmother's house for dinner. I hated the trip and getting dressed up, though I loved her and her meatballs. The sauce, the lasagne, the sausages—everything was good. But I remember the meatballs. So my mother started to make them. That's when I discovered still another dimension to meatballs. At my grandmother's the meatballs were already fixed and soaking in the tomato sauce. But at home I could drift into the kitchen and steal one or two before they were plunged into the sauce. Soon I came to eat so many that my Mom, a competitive lady, would prepare huge quantities, so as not to be bested by my appetite. It was at this point that I made still another discovery, I liked cold, leftover fried meatballs without sauce. I liked them even more after running over to the cheese store and purchasing fresh homemade water mozzarella, alternating a bite of each. This remains one of my childhood's fondest memories, which I am pleased to share."

> 4 stale seedless bread rolls
> 1½ pounds ground top sirloin
> ½ pound ground pork
> 5 whole eggs
> ¾ cup freshly grated Parmesan cheese
> 1 tablespoon fresh chopped parsley
> 1 teaspoon salt
> freshly ground pepper to taste
> ½ cup vegetable oil

Break rolls into pieces and place in a bowl. Cover with water until soaked through. With your hand squeeze out all water and place in a fresh large bowl. Add remaining ingredients. Mix throughly with your hand until smooth. Shape into meatballs the size of a handball. Now heat oil until quite hot but not smoking and add meatballs. Fry until crispy brown all over. Turn gently with large spoon as the various sides brown. When completely crisp, remove and drain. Meatballs can be added to favorite sauce or eaten as is. They are good as an appetizer or cold the next day with mozzarella, which Ken thinks is one of the Seven Wonders of the World.

INSTANT NEW ENGLAND CLAM CHOWDER

While daddy's watching the kids he is not going to have time to open clams, so here's a simple version of the clam lover's favorite hot soup. Let the kids open the cans.

>   2 10¾-ounce cans cream of potato soup
>   2 cans milk (use empty soup can for measurement)
>   2 8-ounce cans minced clams and juice
>   ¼ teaspoon dried thyme
>   ½ teaspoon seasoned salt
>   freshly ground pepper
>   butter

Place all ingredients except butter in pot and stir well. Bring to a near boil, reduce heat and simmer for 10 minutes. On top of each bowl of soup add a pat of butter. Serve with oyster crackers, which children of all ages love.

>   Serves 6.

This soup is an easy one to prepare on a boat or to take along in a thermos for an outing.

CREAMED CHIPPED BEEF

When I was a girl in Kansas, creamed chipped beef was a meal we had about once a week. I loved it and thought my mother was an absolute genius to be able to make it. She always laughs about that since it was one of our economy meals and so easy to prepare. Many men tell me they often get a craving for some good chipped beef at the strangest times. I think it's a nice change for a hearty breakfast or brunch. And the kids will love it.

>   4 tablespoons butter
>   2 tablespoons flour
>   1½ cups milk, heated
>   6-ounce jar dried beef (soak in water to cover for 20
>   minutes and drain well before using, to reduce salty
>   taste)
>   1 8-ounce can green peas, drained
>   freshly ground pepper

Melt butter in saucepan. Sprinkle flour over butter and stir with whisk. Slowly pour heated milk into mixture (called a roux), whisking constantly until sauce has thickened and is smooth. Add drained dried beef and green peas. Gently blend. Stir over medium heat until throughly heated. Season well with freshly ground pepper. Salt may be needed, but that will depend on the saltiness of the beef, so taste and see.

Serve over toast or sliced boiled potatoes and garnish with fresh chopped parsley.

Serves 3 or 4.

MACARONI AND CHEESE

Macaroni and cheese is an economical and nutritious meal. Served with a simple green vegetable or salad, it's a dish sure to be devoured by all.

> *8 ounces elbow macaroni*
> *3 tablespoons butter*
> *3 tablespoons flour*
> *1½ cups milk, heated*
> *½ teaspoon salt*
> *freshly ground pepper to taste*
> *½ teaspoon dry mustard*
> *1 cup shredded Cheddar cheese*
> *1 medium onion, chopped*
> *2 tablespoons butter*

Boil macaroni according to package directions. Drain in colander. Meanwhile, prepare sauce: in saucepan melt butter and stir in flour. Cook over medium-low heat for a minute, stirring. Slowly pour heated milk into mixture, stirring constantly, until sauce has thickened. Season with salt, pepper and mustard. Add cheese and stir until melted. Saute onion in butter for 4 minutes and add to sauce. Pour macaroni into buttered 2½-quart baking dish. Pour sauce over macaroni. Bake in preheated 350 F. oven for about 25 minutes, until top is lightly browned.

Serves 4.

JACK YOGMAN'S TAMALE JIVE

Vice-chairman of Esquire, Inc., Jack Yogman is an executive whose travels have enabled him to explore all manner of food throughout the world. His experiences have left him with a "When in Rome" philosophy. In other words, he doesn't order corned beef hash on the Via Veneto. Jack often cooks for his family and he gave me two of his recipes that are family favorites. I can see why. I tested both Tamale Jive and his Meat Loaf, which follows, and found myself eating far too many portions. His recipes are uncomplicated to prepare and most original in flavor. They are just the sort of recipes to use when you want to wean the teenagers from pizza and hamburger.

1 tablespoon vegetable oil
1 1/2 pounds ground beef
1 medium-large onion, chopped
1 large green pepper (or green chile pepper), chopped
3 cups peeled chopped tomatoes
3 cups kernel corn, canned or cooked (drained)
1 teaspoon salt
freshly ground pepper to taste
1 tablespoon chili powder (or to taste)
1/2 teaspoon dried oregano
2 cups boiling water
1 1/2 cups yellow corn meal
2 dozen pitted black olives
paprika

Heat oil in large skillet or pot. Saute ground beef, onion and pepper until meat loses pink color, stirring often. Add tomatoes, corn, salt, pepper, chili powder and oregano. Mix and simmer for 20 minutes. Into boiling water, quickly mix corn meal and thoroughly combine corn meal and meat mixture. Turn into large casserole dish. Press olives into mixture, making sure mixture covers olives, and sprinkle with paprika. Bake, covered, in preheated 325 F. oven for 1 hour (uncovered, bake 30 minutes).

Serves 6 to 8.

This casserole is even better if reheated the next day.

JACK YOGMAN'S MEAT LOAF

¾ pound ground beef
¾ pound ground veal
1 medium onion, grated
1 green pepper, chopped
1 tablespoon capers
2 tablespoons raisins
8 stuffed green olives, chopped
1 tablespoon ketchup
½ teaspoon dry mustard
1½ teaspoons fresh chopped parsley
½ teaspoon salt
freshly ground pepper to taste
1 egg
½ cup milk
⅔ cup cornflake crumbs
1 tablespoon flour
paprika
1 tablespoon vegetable oil
garlic clove, peeled and halved

Mix all ingredients but flour, paprika, vegetable oil and garlic. Shape into loaf and place in loaf pan. Sprinkle top with flour, then paprika. Brush with oil. Add ½ inch of water to pan with garlic pieces. Bake in preheated 350 F. oven for 1 to 1½ hours depending on your preference for doneness.

Serves 6.

Also excellent the next day.

FUNNY HOT DOGS

Here are a few ways to make hot dogs a little more enticing than the usual hot dogs and mustard. Boil frankfurters in water or score them and saute in butter until golden or grill them on the barbecue. Butter hot dog buns and brown lightly under the broiler.

Place cooked hot dogs on toasted buns and top with any of the following ingredients:

Canned caponata.

Ratatouille (see recipe in index).

Heated chili topped with minced raw onion, green pepper and parsley.

Melted American cheese and crumbled bacon.

Crisp fried onion rings and shredded cheese. Place under broiler until cheese melts.

A whole scallion and hot potato salad.

Chopped sauteed tomatoes, sprinkled with oregano and diced mozzarella cheese. Brown under broiler.

Onions and green peppers sauteed in a little oil.

Baked beans, corn relish and thinly sliced red onion rings.

All the above can be served with potato chips, French fries or mixed green salad.

DAD'S PEANUT BUTTER COOKIES

Part of the fun in cooking with children is to let them take an active part in the pleasures of measuring, mixing and arranging a dish. What better fun could a father and child have than baking cookies and being able to surprise mom with a full cookie jar.

½ cup butter, softened
½ cup peanut butter
1 egg
½ cup granulated sugar
½ cup brown sugar
1¼ cups all-purpose flour
½ teaspoon baking soda
½ teaspoon baking powder
¼ teaspoon salt

In a large bowl mix butter, peanut butter, egg, sugar and brown sugar. Sift remaining dry ingredients and stir into peanut butter mixture. Chill dough for half an hour, then roll dough into spheres the size of a walnut. Place each on greased baking sheet about 3 inches apart. Flatten each ball with the back of a fork dipped lightly in flour to prevent sticking. Make a criss-cross design while flattening the top of the cookies. Bake in preheated 375 F. oven for 10 to 12 minutes.

Yield: 3 dozen cookies.

BACHELOR MEALS

A SINGLE MAN'S CHICKEN BREAST

1 large chicken breast, split in half (Cut along center of chicken breast and remove breast bone and cartilage, or have your butcher split it for you.)
salt and pepper
2 tablespoons flour
1 tablespoon vegetable oil
2 tablespoons butter
2 tablespoons Marsala
⅓ cup heavy cream
1 teaspoon freshly chopped parsley

Season chicken breast with salt and pepper. Coat with flour. Heat oil and butter in small frying pan large enough to comfortably hold chicken. Cook chicken over medium heat for about 6 minutes until lightly browned, turn and cook 6 minutes more. Add Marsala and turn chicken. Bring to a boil. Add cream and when it bubbles, serve, garnished with parsley.

Serve over hot fluffy rice with a side dish of green peas or Carrots Vichy.

Serves 1.

ROCK CORNISH GAME HEN FOR ONE

1 rock cornish game hen
salt and pepper
1 small onion
2 strips bacon
2 tablespoons butter, melted

Season cavity of bird with salt and pepper. Chop onion in half and place inside bird. Tie legs together with string and fold wings back. Place bird on rack in small roasting pan with ½ inch of water. Cut strips of bacon in half and place over breast of bird. Place in 425 F. preheated oven and roast for 10 minutes. Reduce heat to 350 F. and cook for 35 more minutes, basting with melted butter occasionally.

Serve with broccoli and baked potato. (Potato should go into the oven the same time as the bird.)

Serves 1.

SOLO CELEBRATION DINNER

There are times when a celebration is in order—a promotion, a raise, an accomplishment of any kind—and you are alone. You might even want to celebrate being alone. Preparing oneself an elegant meal can be very satisfying, to say nothing of its therapeutic value. During the work in the kitchen, dress in comfortable clothes, play favorite music and don't answer the phone. Dine by candlelight at the table using your best dinnerware, crystal and silver. A fresh cloth napkin is a must.

> 2 ounces Beluga caviar
> 3 slices toast, crust trimmed, toast cut in half
>   diagonally
>
> split of champagne
>
> Filet mignon
> 6 fresh asparagus spears with lemon butter
> Endive and arugula salad with vinaigrette sauce
>
> red wine
>
> Vanilla ice cream with sliced fresh peach and Gran
>   Marnier
>
> cognac

See index for recipes.

OYSTERS LINDBERG

Fresh oysters shivering deliciously in a little lemon juice are taste miracles of nature. Since they aren't cooked, it is only necessary to learn the correct way to open and serve them. After scrubbing oysters under cold water, hold them in one hand with a cloth napkin or small towel with the flat side of shell on top. Insert an oyster knife (a knife with a short, strong, sharp blade with a strong handle) into hinge of shell. Twist the knife to cut muscle. Then run knife between shells and pry open over a bowl to save any juice which may fall out. Arrange 6, or as many oysters as you have appetite for, in a large plate 2 inches deep, filled with crushed ice. (Discard any oysters which don't close tightly during handling.)

Serve oysters with juice accumulated in bowl and lemon wedges.

(If you must, accompany oysters with cocktail sauce and horseradish, but remember that these strong condiments mask the delicate flavor of the oyster.)

Serves 1.

CELEBRATION BREAKFAST FOR TWO

MENU:
Mimosa
Scrambled Eggs with Caviar
Toast Points with Butter
Strawberries with Crème Fraîche
Café au Lait
(No Newspapers!)

MIMOSA:
Mix equal amounts of champage with orange juice. Both should be well chilled.

SCRAMBLED EGGS WITH CAVIAR:

5 eggs
¼ teaspoon seasoned salt
3 tablespoons butter

> 3 tablespoons heavy cream
> 3 ounces caviar

Mix eggs in bowl with seasoned salt. Heat butter in skillet and add eggs. Gently turn eggs with tablespoon for a few seconds. Pour cream over eggs and continue to slowly turn eggs. When cooked to desired doneness remove to serving bowl and top with caviar.

CAFÉ AU LAIT:

Pour equal amounts of hot coffee and scalded milk into oversized coffee cups. Add sugar if used.

JOHN DRUCKER'S BACHELOR MEAL FOR TWO

Though John Drucker owns a lamp manufacturing company in Georgia, he prefers candlelight at dinner time. "It's very relaxing." His favorite dish is duck and his favorite recipe is "A little blonde in the kitchen." He's been charged with sexist remarks before, but simply states he likes good food with good company. If she can't cook, he'll be happy to roast the duck and light the candles. Here is John's duck dinner for two.

MENU:
Roast Duck
Broccoli (see index for recipe)
Seasoned Rice
Tossed Salad
Chocolate Ice Cream

ROAST DUCK:

> 4-pound duck
> salt and pepper
> 2 cups water
> 1 medium onion, chopped
> 1 carrot, chopped
> 2 stalks celery, chopped
> ¼ teaspoon dried thyme
> 1 cup dry white wine

Remove giblets from duck and save. Season duck inside and out with salt and pepper. Place in roasting pan with 1 cup water. Roast in preheated 425 F. oven for 45 minutes. Reduce heat to 400 F. Cook about 45 minutes longer. Place giblets—neck, gizzard and heart—of duck in saucepan with onion, carrot, celery, thyme, 1 cup water and white wine. Bring to a boil and then simmer over low heat for 45 minutes to 1 hour. Strain stock. When duck has cooked remove from roasting pan. Pour stock into the pan where duck roasted. Bring to a boil. Check seasoning and strain. Cut duck in half and remove backbone. Place duck on serving dish and pour sauce over it.

SEASONED RICE:
1 cup raw long-grain rice
2½ cups water
2 beef bouillon cubes
pinch of thyme
2 scallions, finely sliced
1 tablespoon butter
salt and freshly ground pepper to taste

Bring water to a boil. Add rice and remaining ingredients. Bring to a boil again, reduce heat, cover and simmer about 25 minutes. Drain. Adjust seasoning.

TOSSED SALAD:

1 small head romaine lettuce
½ cup bean sprouts, drained

DRESSING:
3 tablespoons olive oil
1 tablespoon lemon juice
1 tablespoon soy sauce
1 clove garlic, crushed
¼ teaspoon dry mustard
¼ teaspoon salt
freshly ground pepper to taste

Break cleaned and dried lettuce leaves into small pieces. Add bean sprouts. Mix dressing together in small bowl and pour over salad and toss just before serving.

LEO BLOOM'S CHICKEN
TENTH AVENUE FOR TWO

Leo Bloom, bachelor actor, confides:

I am compelled—for my own social survival—to assume a pretense of uninterrupted affluence, and learned to do so through the deft manipulation of my pots and pans. As I have created illusion in the theater, so have I learned to do in my dining room. When I'm successful, my modest Tenth Avenue address is dismissed as a quaint anomaly, as one views tattered blue jeans on the rich. If diamonds are a girl's best friend, then a good meal properly appointed may persuade her that real gems cannot be far behind. It probably never occurred to Frank Perdue, but what basic black is to those with sartorial concerns, basic chicken is to the kitchen roué. The following recipe may be readily modified to accommodate particular personality traits of the guest, if not the chicken. For example, if she is extroverted and adventuresome one may add ginger. Should she evince erotic predilections behind a monasterial air, add wine generously in the marinade, in the sauce, in the guest.

A word about wine. There is an old Chinese saying which, freely translated, cautions: when dining in a poor neighborhood never drink wine from a decanter; it may be embracing a cheap product. In practice any wine will do, but it must be poured from a bottle whose label contains no intelligible English. Classically, French is the choice, but vintage '76 Serbo-Croatian may render her equally awestruck. The bottle should be carefully sprinkled with household soot, which is casually displayed as wine cellar dust. And it must rest in a cradle, whether sterling or papier mâché, no more than thirty degrees from the horizontal plane. No less important are napkin rings and appropriate chicken music. And never, never use a single candle. That is for pizza in cold-water flats. George Jensen Candelabra and Woolworth candles will effectively portray you as a man of means and humility—a winning combination.

Keep uppermost in mind that image must be meticulously pursued, which in consort with taste, are mutually augmenting. In summation, serve chicken, but think pheasant.

For the purist this creation can be savored for its own sake; for the swinging chef it can, if history is any lesson, be a means to an end. Properly executed, you will never get to serve dessert. And, weight watchers, a blessing; this dish is not fattening.

3 ½-pound roasting chicken
2 tablespoons margarine
4 scallions, chopped
¼ cup soy sauce
3 tablespoons melted margarine

Heat margarine and saute scallions for 5 minutes, stirring often. Add soy sauce and remove from heat. Place chicken in deep ceramic or glass dish and pour sauce over chicken, cover and refrigerate for 6 hours. Baste chicken with sauce several times during this time. Remove chicken to roasting pan on rack. Mix 3 tablespoons melted butter with marinade. Brush chicken with mixture. Place chicken in preheated 350 F. oven for about 1 hour and 10 minutes (20 minutes per pound). Baste two or three times during cooking. Remove chicken when done. Allow it to rest for 5 minutes. Cut in half, remove backbone and place each half on warm dinner plates. Pour remaining marinade over chicken.

Serves 2.

CAESAR SALAD

A mouth-watering delicious Caesar Salad tossed at the table makes an impressive light entree for a bachelor dinner. Simply accompany with French bread and a dry white wine. For dessert, a generous wedge of brie with a fresh pear or apple—and invite me.

2 cloves garlic
1 medium head romaine lettuce, cleaned, crisped and
      broken into bite-size pieces
¼ cup olive oil
¼ teaspoon dry mustard
¼ teaspoon salt
freshly ground pepper to taste
juice of large juicy lemon, strained
1 teaspoon Worcestershire sauce
6 anchovy filets
1 egg, boiled in shell for 1 minute
1 cup fried croutons (See index for recipe.)
¼ cup freshly grated Parmesan cheese

Peel garlic cloves, cut in half and rub garlic over bottom and sides of salad bowl, and add lettuce. Have remaining ingredients assembled on tray on table. Sprinkle lettuce with olive oil, dry mustard, salt, pepper and lemon juice. Toss gently. Add Worcestershire sauce, anchovies and egg. Toss again until salad is evenly coated. Sprinkle croutons and Parmesan cheese over salad and toss once more. Serve immediately.

Serves 2.

TOM RICHMOND'S BACHELOR
DINNER FOR TWO

Tom Richmond, a fellow Kansan, a bachelor, and a public relations man, has lived in New York for many years. He loves good food, frequents New York's finest restaurants and appreciates the grape. He is a self-taught cook. In his early quest for instruction he purchased an advanced cookbook with menus and slowly worked his way through every menu in the book. He recalls a hot July day when he spent the entire morning shopping and six hours in his small hot kitchen preparing a rather complicated meal from the book. He lost a few pounds, he says, but produced a winner. Tom does not lack ambition when planning a dinner party. He relishes selecting everything from the tablecloth, flowers, china and wine glasses, etc., to shopping for all the food; in several stores, if necessary. Then he leisurely cooks the meal.

Several years ago he came up with the idea of using old pictures of friends attending the dinner instead of place cards.

His favorite appetizer is smoked salmon with the usual capers and lemon, but the lemon must be wrapped in cheesecloth, so juice or seeds won't spurt out on the guest.

Here is the menu and recipes he suggests men might use to make a nice dinner "that won't kill you" for a date after work.

MENU:
Smoked Salmon
Broiled Sole with Mushrooms in Wine Sauce
Poached and Sauteed Zucchini
Tomato and Basil Salad
Blueberry Tart

SMOKED SALMON:

½ pound smoked salmon
2 tablespoons capers
1 lemon, cut in half and wrapped in small piece of
    doubled cheesecloth

Arrange thinly sliced salmon in two serving plates. Sprinkle salmon with capers and place lemon on side of each dish. Serve with fresh toast, crusts removed.

BROILED SOLE WITH MUSHROOMS IN WINE SAUCE:

2 medium filets of sole
1 teaspoon lemon juice
salt and pepper
¼ teaspoon dried dill weed
2 tablespoons butter
paprika
¼ pound thinly sliced mushrooms
½ cup dry white wine

Sprinkle sole filets with lemon juice. Season with salt and pepper and dill weed. Fold each filet in half. Place in shallow baking dish. Put 1 tablespoon of butter on each filet. Sprinkle with paprika. Surround with sliced mushrooms and pour in wine. Broil 6 inches from heat for about 6 minutes. Stir mushrooms, gently. Continue to cook for about 6 to 8 minutes more until sole flakes easily (no need to turn fish).

POACHED AND SAUTEED ZUCCHINI:

2 medium zucchini
2½ cups water
salt and pepper to taste
2 tablespoons butter
1 tablespoon parsley

Peel zucchini and slice each in half lengthwise. Then cut each half in half lengthwise. With small sharp knife cut away seeds in center of zucchini. Slice zucchini into 1-inch lengths. Bring water to a boil. Season with salt and pepper. Drop zucchini into boiling water, cover and simmer for 6 minutes. Drain. Melt butter in small skillet and add zucchini and saute for 5 minutes, turning zucchini once or twice gently with spatula. Check seasoning and sprinkle with fresh chopped parsley.

TOMATO AND BASIL SALAD:

> 1 large beefsteak tomato, thinly sliced
> 6 leaves fresh basil or ½ teaspoon dried basil
> ⅓ cup Vinaigrette Dressing (See index for recipe.)

Arrange tomato slices on two salad plates. Sprinkle with chopped or dried basil. Pour Vinaigrette Dressing over tomatoes and refrigerate until ready to dine.

BLUEBERRY TART:

> 1 9-inch pie crust dough (see desserts for recipe)
> 1 pint blueberries, washed and picked
> 4 tablespoons sugar
> 2 tablespoons butter

Roll dough and place in 9-inch tart flan ring. Sprinkle 2 tablespoons of sugar over crust. Add blueberries and distribute evenly over surface. Sprinkle top with remaining 2 tablespoons sugar and dot with butter. Place in preheated 425 F. oven and bake for 45 minutes. Cool before serving.

There's plenty of the blueberry tart left over for the next day.

DAVID HARTMAN'S CHICKEN

David Hartman, actor and host of the "Good Morning America" show, loves food. I've cooked dishes on the show several times at 7:45 a.m., and even at that hour David is always anxious to eat anything from marinated mussels to a rich dessert. Before he married several years ago, his favorite bachelor dish was one he invented with chicken breasts and pineapple and grapefruit juice. Now, he considers it a boring entree (no wonder: he admits to preparing it at least a thousand times). But it is great tasting and, after two easy steps, you just turn the oven on and wait to smell the juice cooking.

Another bachelor favorite of David's is to bake a few halved chicken breasts with commercially packaged Noodles Romanoff. Use package directions for preparation and timing.

Here's the juice recipe:

> 4 chicken breasts, halved
> 2 tablespoons melted butter
> salt and freshly ground pepper, to taste
> 2 cups pineapple juice and grapefruit juice mixture

Brush chicken breasts with butter and sprinkle with salt and pepper. Place in buttered shallow baking dish skin-side-up. Pour juice over chicken and bake in preheated 350 F. oven for 50 minutes.

> Serves 4.

BILL MURFIN'S MOUSSAKA

Bill Murfin loves to cook and eagerly considers what or where dinner will be as soon as he gets up each morning.

"I guess there are as many recipes for Moussaka as there are Greeks. I've yet to find one that I think equals this one. I can't recall how or where I got it, so I just take the credit myself."

> 1 large eggplant
> ¼ cup olive oil
> 2 medium onions, chopped
> 2 cloves garlic, minced
> 1 pound groud lamb or beef
> 1 teaspoon salt
> ½ teaspoon dried thyme
> ½ teaspoon dried oregano
> ½ teaspoon nutmeg
> ½ teaspoon cinnamon
> 2 tablespoons fresh chopped parsley
> 1 cup canned tomatoes, chopped
> ½ cup dry white wine
> ½ cup dry bread crumbs, plain or seasoned

SAUCE:

3 tablespoons butter
3 tablespoons flour
1½ cups milk, heated
2 egg yolks
½ teaspoon salt
pepper to taste
1 whole egg
4 teaspoons grated Parmesan cheese

Peel eggplant and cut into ½-inch-thick slices, sprinkle with salt and allow to sit for ½ hour. Meanwhile, heat 2 tablespoons olive oil and brown meat with onions and garlic. Drain. Return to pan and add salt, seasonings, parsley, tomatoes and wine. Cover and simmer for 30 minutes. Prepare sauce. Melt butter in saucepan and add flour, whisking constantly. Slowly stir in hot milk until sauce thickens. Remove from heat. Add egg yolks, salt and pepper. When meat mixture has cooked remove from heat and let cool, then mix in whole egg and half the bread crumbs. Rinse eggplant and pat dry. In clean skillet, heat rest of olive oil and saute eggplant slices until lightly browned on each side. Add more oil, if necessary. Sprinkle bottom of greased 11 by 14-inch rectangular baking dish with remaining bread crumbs. Cover with eggplant. Pour sauce over top and sprinkle with Parmesan cheese. Bake in preheated 350 F. oven for 45 minutes.

Serves 4.

FONDUE BOURGUIGNONNE

Beef fondue means entertaining. It's become increasingly popular in the past decade in America, but Switzerland has been savoring cheese fondue (Neuchateloise) for years; beef fondue has been a favorite there long enough for the actual origin to be a matter of question.

The dish is stimulating fare for a party of six or, as I prefer, a party of two.

Serve with several sauces. My favorites are: Béarnaise, Curry, Rémoulade.* Some sauces can be prepared well ahead of time. Serve beef fondue with a crisp tossed salad and red wine.

*See index for sauce recipes.

FONDUE EQUIPMENT:
Fondue Pot (Stainless steel or copper)
Denatured alcohol
Fondue forks
Fondue plates (optional) or individual sauce dishes

3 pounds beef filet
3½ cups vegetable or peanut oil or enough to fill pot
half full

Cut beef into 1½-inch cubes and pile into platter. Heat oil in pot until it bubbles when you place piece of beef in it. Serve guests beef cubes and sauces. Each guest fixes piece of beef on fork and places it in oil in pot for about 3 minutes or until desired doneness.

Serves 6.

CHEESE FONDUE

1½ cups dry white wine
1 pound Gruyère or Swiss cheese
¼ cup flour
pinch nutmeg, freshly grated
freshly ground pepper to taste
1 loaf crusty French bread, cut into 1-inch cubes (bread
can be lightly toasted in oven, if desired)

Heat wine in enamel saucepan. Shred cheese and toss with flour. Stir mixture into wine. Season with nutmeg and pepper. Stir until cheese has melted. Pour into fondue dish or chafing dish and place over Sterno. Serve with bowls of bread cubes. Long cocktail picks or fondue forks should be provided.

Serves 4.

STUFFED GREEN PEPPERS

4 large green peppers
½ pound ground pork
½ pound ground beef
1 cup cooked rice
1 small onion, minced
1 small garlic clove, crushed
1 teaspoon salt
freshly ground pepper to taste
2 8-ounce cans tomato sauce
1 teaspoon paprika
1 tablespoon sugar
2 teaspoons lemon juice
½ teaspoon salt

Cut tops off peppers and remove seeds. Boil in water to cover
them for 5 minutes and drain. Mix pork, beef, rice, onion, garlic
and salt and pepper. Fill peppers with mixture and place in baking dish just large enough to hold peppers. Mix remaining ingredients and pour over peppers. Cover and place in preheated 350 F.
oven for 45 minutes.

Serves 4.

CHILI

I don't know of a single man who doesn't love chili. There are so
many prize-winning recipes available with varying ingredients.
Here's my own contribution, which I first served at an after-
theater outdoor dinner party at the Goodspeed Opera House in
East Haddam, Connecticut. I encourage you to create your own
variation.

1 pound ground beef
1 medium-large onion, chopped
1 green pepper, seeded and chopped
2 tablespoons chili powder
1 teaspoon cumin
1 teaspoon salt

freshly ground pepper
2 1-pound cans kidney beans and liquid
1 1-pound can whole tomatoes and liquid
2 cups water
2 beef bouillon cubes
1 tablespoon Worcestershire sauce
pinch cayenne pepper

In large pot saute ground beef, onion and green pepper until meat is no longer pink. Stir this mixture often. Add remaining ingredients and bring to a boil. Reduce heat and simmer for 1 hour.

Serve with shredded lettuce and onions, and cornbread.

Serves 6.

JACK HARROLD'S TACO CASSEROLE

Jack Harrold, a voice teacher, actor and singer, has a passion for music and good food. He and his long-time friend, opera star Zinka Milanov, have cooking competitions, and he's constantly practicing his culinary prowess to come up with the winner.

1½ pounds ground beef
1 large onion, chopped
1 large green pepper, seeded and chopped
½ teaspoon salt
freshly ground pepper to taste
1 tablespoon chili powder
½ teaspoon dried basil
3 cups taco chips
2 1-pound cans red kidney beans, drained
1 8-ounce can taco sauce

Saute ground beef, onion and green pepper until meat loses pink color, stirring often. Sprinkle with salt, pepper, chili powder and basil. Blend well. In large casserole dish, arrange layer of beef mixture over bottom of dish, a layer of taco chips, a layer of kidney beans and repeat, ending with a layer of taco chips. Pour taco sauce over top and bake in preheated 325 F. oven for 30 minutes.

Serve with shredded lettuce and scallions.

Serves 6 to 8.

ARTHUR HERZOG'S CHOUCROUTE GARNIE
[For a party]

Arthur Herzog, author of The Swarm *and many other books, warned me I'd need an enormous platter, patience and a healthy appetite for this dish. I assured him I had all those requisites. Arthur lived in France for a while and Choucroute Garnie became a favorite dish. A resourceful man, he found the recipe in a cookbook and learned how to make it. He recited the recipe to me from memory, so I could write it down. "It's a gorgeous thing to serve to a crowd of people."*

When Arthur's invited to a private home for a "gourmet dinner" he shudders, because, he says, in his experience such meals are never very successful. He prefers more uncomplicated dishes for home-cooked meals. I have invited Arthur to attend a "sophisticated meal" in my home to try and disprove his theory. It is going to be a challenge because Arthur is a fine food critic.

> 5 pounds fresh sauerkraut (available in plastic bags in
>   your supermarket)
> 2 ounces salt pork or bacon
> 2 large onions, sliced
> 1 teaspoon caraway seeds
> 8 peppercorns
> 6 juniper berries (optional)
> 2½ pounds sliced smoked pork butt
> 2 pounds thick slices of smoked ham
> 8 knockwurst or kielbasa, cut into 1½-inch lengths
> 3 cups water
> 2 cups dry white wine
> 4 pounds potatoes, cooked, peeled and cut into large
>   chunks (the potatoes should be cooked just before
>   serving with dish)

The most important step in making Choucroute Garnie is rinsing the sauerkraut. It must be soaked in 3 different waters and allowed to rest 5 minutes in each fresh water bath. After the last soaking, take a fresh dish towel and dry several strands of sauerkraut at a time. This is time consuming, so get your guests to help you and turn work into fun. Place diced pork salt or bacon in large pot or kettle and cook until fat is rendered. Add onions and cook for 10 minutes over medium low heat. Add sauerkraut, caraway seeds, peppercorns, and juniper berries. Stir to combine well.

Pour in water and wine. Bring to a boil, reduce heat and simmer for 10 minutes.

In large casserole transfer enough sauerkraut mixture to generously cover bottom of dish. Add sliced pork butt, then add another layer of sauerkraut mixture. Next, place pieces of smoked ham over top and, again, sauerkraut. Add knockwurst or kielbasa and top with remaining sauerkraut. Bake in preheated 325 F. oven for 1½ hours or simmer on top of stove. Arrange sauerkraut in center of huge platter and top with neatly arranged meat. Place boiled potatoes around meat.

For a festive touch serve 3 different kinds of mustard with dish, along with a green salad and French bread. Carafes of red wine, too.

Serves 16.

DIET DISHES

It is difficult to have thin thoughts when what you crave is pizza with sausage and extra cheese, French fries or a huge slice of chocolate cake. "Put anything you want in your mouth, just don't swallow it." Will power is the only answer. Will power and non-fattening foods.

If your reaction to rabbit food (raw asparagus, carrots, celery, green pepper, salads, etc.) is negative, then be more creative. Try a piece of cheese and an apple or pear. Try half a grapefruit. Try a small pickle. Try a diet soda. Try a huge glass of club soda in an attractive glass filled with ice and a lemon slice. Try a hard-boiled egg, or try any of the following recipes!

ONE DAY 900 CALORIE DIET MENU

BREAKFAST:

8 ounces tomato juice with juice of 1 wedge of fresh
    lemon

1 poached egg on 1 slice of wholewheat bread*

1 cup coffee or tea, black or with tablespoon of skim
    milk

LUNCH:

1 3½-ounce can white meat tuna packed in water
1 tomato, sliced
2 stalks celery
1 large glass of iced tea with lemon but no sugar
      (use sugar substitute if necessary)

DINNER:

½ small broiled chicken*
6 stalks boiled asparagus*
salad composed of 1 cup lettuce pieces, ½ small cu-
      cumber, sliced, and a dressing made with 1 ta-
      blespoon wine vinegar, salt, pepper and ¼ tea
      spoon dried basil
1 4-ounce glass dry white wine
1 fresh peach or pear

CANTALOUPE WITH BLUEBERRIES

2 cantaloupes, cut in half and seeded
2 cups fresh blueberries
½ pint sour cream
4 tablespoons brown sugar

In center of each cantaloupe place ½ cup blueberries, ¼ cup sour cream, and top with tablespoon brown sugar.

Serves 4.

MELON AND PROSCIUTTO

Late-night heavy food should always be avoided, but if the hunger pains are winning the battle, a generous slice of fresh ripe melon with several paper-thin slices of prosciutto is an excellent light meal.

As an appetizer, cut melon into small cubes, wrap with a thin piece of prosciutto and secure with a toothpick. If you don't have prosciutto handy, substitute thinly sliced boiled ham pieces.

*For recipe, see index.

YOGHURT AND FRUIT

1 cup yoghurt
4 large strawberries, sliced
½ cup fresh blueberries

Combine ingredients. If you like yoghurt sweetened, use a sugar substitute.

Serves 1.

FRESH BOILED BEETS

1 bunch beets
salt and freshly ground pepper
vinegar

Cut tops from beets, leaving about 2 inches of stem attached to prevent beets from bleeding. Place in boiling lightly salted water to cover them and cook for about 40 minutes or until tender. This will depend on their size. Cut off stems and slice beets in thin slices. Serve with plenty of freshly ground pepper and a splash of vinegar.

Serves 4.

CARROTS WITH MINT

1 pound carrots, peeled and cut diagonally into 1-inch
  pieces
1 chicken bouillon cube
1 tablespoon freshly chopped mint or ½ teaspoon dried
  mint
1 tablespoon butter

Bring about two cups of lightly salted water to a boil. Add carrots and bouillon cube. Cover and cook over medium heat for 10 minutes until carrots are done but still crisp. Drain and add mint and butter. Toss gently until butter melts and serve immediately.

Serves 4.

BROILED TOMATOES

4 tomatoes
¼ cup low-calorie Italian dressing
¼ teaspoon dried basil
1 tablespoon dried bread crumbs

Cut stem ends off tomatoes. With teaspoon remove tomato pulp and place in bowl. Mix with dressing, basil and salt and pepper. Refill tomatoes. Sprinkle lightly with bread crumbs and broil until golden on top.

Serves 4.

BROILED CHICKEN

½ broiling chicken (A broiling chicken is simply a
chicken which weighs 1½ to 2½ pounds; a frying
chicken weighs 2 to 3½ pounds.)
1 teaspoon vegetable oil plus ½ teaspoon lemon or lime
juice
seasoned salt

Heat gas or electric broiler in your stove. Place chicken in broiling pan. Brush each side with combined oil and lemon or lime juice and sprinkle lightly with seasoned salt. Place chicken on rack in pan about 6 or 7 inches under broiler, bone-side-up. Cook 12 to 14 minutes. Turn and cook about the same time on skin side, watching so that chicken doesn't burn. If you find your broiler is very hot and chicken is cooking too fast, lower oven rack an inch or two.

For variety brush broiler with any of the following combinations:

1 tablespoon vegetable oil	1 tablespoon vegetable oil
1 teaspoon lemon juice	1 tablespoon soy sauce
¼ teaspoon oregano	1 teaspoon grated onion
freshly ground pepper	freshly ground pepper

1 tablespoon vegetable oil
1 teaspoon lemon juice
pinch of curry powder
½ teaspoon dried tarragon
freshly ground pepper

1 tablespoon vegetable oil
1 clove garlic, crushed
1 tablespoon red wine
1 teaspoon finely chopped parsley
freshly ground pepper

Serves 1.

TUNA PLATE

2 crisp leaves lettuce
1 3½-ounce can water-packed tuna (drained)
2 thin slices cantaloupe
½ medium tomato, cut into wedges
4 slices cucumber
2 stalks raw asparagus, washed, tough ends trimmed off
1 small scoop low-fat cottage cheese

Place lettuce leaves on plate. Arrange tuna, cantaloupe, tomato wedges, cucumber slices and asparagus on lettuce. Top tuna with scoop of cottage cheese.

Serves 1.

BROILED SALMON STEAKS
WITH DILL DRESSING

4 1-inch thick salmon steaks
1 tablespoon vegetable oil
2 tablespoons lemon juice
paprika

Place salmon steaks in lightly greased broiling pan. Brush with oil. Sprinkle with lemon juice and paprika. Broil until browned on both sides, about 5 minutes per side.

DRESSING:

⅔ cup diet cottage cheese
3 tablespoons skim milk
1 scallion, chopped
1 teaspoon lemon juice
1 teaspoon fresh dill weed
¼ teaspoon salt
plenty of freshly ground pepper to taste

Puree mixture in blender. Spoon over salmon steaks.

Serves 4

FLOUNDER POACHED IN WINE

4 small flounder filets
½ cup dry white wine
½ cup water
1 small onion, chopped
¼ teaspoon dried tarragon
¼ teaspoon salt

Place filets in lightly greased shallow baking dish. Add remaining ingredients and bake in preheated 350 F. oven for about 20 minutes until fish flakes easily.

Serve with fresh cooked asparagus and lemon wedges.

Serves 4.

THE ULTIMATE MEAL

What prompts me to add this final section is insatiable curiosity about the food preferences different men have. I asked several food-worldly men what dishes they would include if composing "The Ultimate Meal." Expense would be no object. Every food, regardless of the season or location, would be available, and so would the finest cook alive to prepare it under perfect conditions. Each man hesitated briefly or for several days before verbalizing just what meal would produce for him the purest satisfaction: "The Ultimate Meal." The responses ranged from Chili and Ice Cold Heineken to Lotte with Watercress, Glace de Homard and Foie Gras Sauce and 1955 Montrachet.

As George Bernard Shaw said, "There is no sincerer love than the love of food."

RUSSELL BANKS, *President of Grow Chemical*

> Cold Striped Bass with Cucumbers
>
> > Pouilly-Fuissé '69
>
> Duckling Elizabeth with Lingonberries (Old Family Recipe)
>
> Watercress and Belgian Endive Salad with Venetia Dressing
>
> > La Tâche 1961
>
> Grand Marnier Soufflé
>
> > Espresso

ABRAHAM BEAME, *Mayor of New York City*

> Consomme
> Filet of Sole Amandine
> Fresh Asparagus
> Sauteed Potatoes
> Green Salad
>
> > Water
>
> Fresh Fruit
>
> > Tea

BILL BEUTEL, *WABC News Anchorman and Correspondent*

EARLY MORNING BREAKFAST

1 Rounded Tablespoon Beluga Caviar with Finely Chopped Hard-Boiled Egg, Onion with Lemon Juice

Crisp Lean Bacon

Two Fresh Eggs cooked in Bacon Drippings (tops basted with drippings)

Jewish or Hungarian Dark Rye Toast with Butter

Large Glass of Fresh Orange Juice

All the Fresh Brewed Black Coffee he can Drink

LAWRENCE S. COHEN, M.D., *Chief of Cardiology, Yale University*

Oysters Bienville

Filet of Sole Stuffed with Crabmeat and Lobster Sauce

Asparagus with Hollandaise Sauce

Belgian Endive and Hearts of Palm Salad with Vinaigrette Sauce

Louis Jadot

Blanc de Blancs

Marron Glacé with Vanilla Ice Cream

Irish Coffee

MAURICE EVANS, *Actor*

Salmon Mousse*

Baked Young Chicken with Sauce Béchamel

Raw Spinach and Mushroom Salad

Crème Caramel

*See index for recipe.

CLAY FELKER, *Publisher*

BREAKFAST

1 quart Raspberries with Sugar and Cream
Fried Scrapple
Two Fried Eggs, basted
Hominy Grits
Scones, drenched in butter

Café au Lait

Comments: "I can only indulge in this meal once
every two years."

BRUCE JAY FRIEDMAN, *Author*

"Wherever I've lived I've always smelled something
terrific cooking down the hall. My idea of the
Ultimate Meal would be for that woman to suddenly
appear with the food so it would no longer be down
the hall."

MILTON GLASER, *Artist and Food Critic*

Carpaccio (paper-thin sliced raw beef) with grated
    Parmesan Cheese, Olive Oil, Lemon Juice and
    Black Pepper
Spaghetti alla Putanesca (A provocative sauce made
    with anchovies, tomatoes, black olives, Par-
    mesan cheese, etc.)

An Old Barolo

Grilled Funghi Porcini (local Umbrian mushrooms)
Peking Duck with Hoisin Sauce, Scallions and Pan-
    cakes
Ovoli E Tartufi Salad (Ovoli are local Umbrian
    mushrooms) including Chopped Celery and
    Grated Gruyère Cheese

Montrachet
San Pellegrino water

Pear Sherbert

Comments: "True Italian cooking is virtually unknown in this country. Milan and the surrounding area, within a two-hour car ride, has the best food in Italy. You can find a restaurant for every region of Italy. There's no guide telling you where they are, so you need to know someone who'll show you. More often than not, these superb restaurants are unmarked and seat no more than twenty."

HENRY GROSSMAN, *Photographer and Opera Singer*

Smoked Salmon with Capers and Lemon
Linguini with White Clam Sauce
Extra thick Lamb Chops, burned on the outside and
    rare on the inside, with a not sweet Mint Jelly
                          Bertani Soave Bolla
Fresh Asparagus, lightly cooked with Butter
Endive and Boston Lettuce Salad with House Dressing from Sea Fare of the Aegean (NYC restaurant)

                            Gevrey-Chambertin
Pearl Tapioca from Horn and Hardart (NYC restaurant)

                            French Coffee

Comments: "I've never had a better tapioca than Horn and Hardart's. If I was unable to get it, I'd like Fresh Raspberries with Devon Cream or Hot Pecan Pie."

CHARLES HOLLERITH, JR, *Theatrical Producer*

Chili with Grated Monterey Jack Cheese
Bermuda Onion Sandwiches on Buttered Rye Bread
                            Ice Cold Heineken
Vanilla Ice Cream with Chocolate Sauce

                            Espresso
Comments: "In spring Shad Roe and in the fall, Corned Beef and Cabbage."

EDWARD KLEBAN, *Lyricist for "A Chorus Line"*

> Oysters
> Asparagus
> Shad
> Strawberries with Cotswold Cream
>
> Comments: "Accompanied by Spring, a bottle of Montrachet, and you-know-who
>> Love before
>> Wit during
>> Theatre after."

DAVID LIEDERMAN, *President of Saucier Associates*

> Fresh Foie Gras with fresh French Bread
> Caviar Rolled in Smoked Salmon
>> 1969 Nuit St. George Blanc
> Broiled Baby Lobster with Lemon Butter
> Lotte with Watercress, Glace de Homard and Foie Gras Sauce
>> 1955 Montrachet
> Roast Chicken Stuffed with Fresh Truffles, Morels and Cepes with Demi-Glace Pan Drippings and Butter Sauce
> Roast Baby Leg of Lamb with Fresh Country Vegetables and Pureed Onion Sauce
>> Magnum of 1949 La Tour
> Peking Duck
>> 1929 Romanée-Conti
> Prawns with Garlic Sauce
> Filet of Beef with Spring Orange Sauce
>> 1899 Lafite
> Rosemary Cake (An 8-layer cake made with hazelnut and almond batter, chocolate cream and crème fraîche, praline cream and butter cream)
> Hot Puff Pastry Pear and Cream Tart
> Fresh Homemade Ice Creams and Sherberts
>> 1921 Château d'Yquem

Chocolate Truffles filled with Praline Chocolate
Tangellos dipped in Chocolate
Butter Cookies

Espresso
Fine de M. Point

Comments: "The ideal meal is one combining
French and Chinese Cuisine. For this elaborate meal
it is necessary to stretch your stomach for weeks in
advance and know where to obtain a line of credit
to pay for it. The meal must be eaten over a period
of seven to eight hours, stretching occasionally."

RICHARD REEVES, *Political Writer*

Hearts of Celery with Green Olives
Venison Steak
Hearts of Lettuce with Vinaigrette Sauce and crum-
bled Roquefort Cheese

St.-Émilion
Château Cheval-Blanc
Cappuccino

Comments: "Never ruin a meal with vegetables."

HAROLD ROBBINS, *Author*

*As I write this, Harold Robbins is in the south of France working on his
next novel. He asked me to contact Paul Kovi, the owner of The Four
Seasons restaurant, for his Ultimate Meal, which he enjoyed at that
restaurant in March en route from California to Europe. I visited Mr.
Kovi, who has graciously elaborated on the Ultimate Meal that is
always served to Harold Robbins as well as a memorable event which
took place in The Four Seasons a few years ago.*

*Mr. Robbins was dining in the restaurant during the Passover holi-
day and he confided to Mr. Kovi that what he'd really like that night
for dinner was matzoh brei (a matzoh omelet), but the chef wasn't familiar with the dish. Mr. Robbins said he happened to make excellent
matzoh brei, so Mr. Kovi furnished him with the ingredients and cook-*

ing equipment. Seated at a nearby table was Joseph E. Levine, the producer, who inquired what was happening. When he was told that Mr. Robbins was going to prepare matzoh brei because he excelled in that dish, Mr. Levine challenged him, asserting he made the best matzoh brei, and the spirited contest began. Mr. Robbins won. His matzoh brei was crisp, Mr. Levine's was a little soggy.

That was the only cooking contest ever held in The Four Seasons and in all probability the last.

Here is Harold Robbins' Ultimate Meal that is shared with anywhere from 3 to 10 friends:

> Caviar Salad—shredded bibb lettuce, caviar (1½ ounces per person) and lemon juice
>
> Dom Pérignon 1969 in magnum served throughout the meal
>
> Whole Roast Filet of Beef with Truffle Sauce
>
> Assorted Fresh Vegetables
>
> Chateau Haut-Brion 1959
>
> Vacherin (meringue cake) with Fresh Raspberry Sherbert and Fresh Raspberries
>
> Frosted Lemon Soufflé with Grand Marnier
>
> Assorted Special Cookies
>
> Cordials and Brandy

Before Mr. Robbins leaves New York, he orders two chocolate velvet cakes, a Four Seasons specialty, and picks them up on the way to the airport to take to his daughter, Adreana. A chocolate velvet cake is Adreana's Ultimate Meal.

ANDRE SOLTNER, *Chef and Owner of Lutèce*

> Asperges Blanches tiède Vinaigrette
>
> Truites Sauvage à la Menthe
>
> Reisling Clos St. Hume
>
> Lapin Farci
>
> Nouilles Fraîche   Chateau Figeac
>
> Chèvre de Marcigny Frais
>
> Taittinger Comtes de Champagne

Sorbet Pamplemousse
Petits Fours

Café
Hennessey Extra Cognac

Comments: Mr. Soltner dreams of this meal because
it is next to impossible to find white asparagus in
this country. The other dishes are family favorites
from Alsace.

MARVIN TRAUB, *President of Bloomingdale's*
INDIAN JASMINE SUPPER

Chicken Pakora
Alu Chaat
Tandoori Chicken
Fish Tikka
Malai Kofta
Lamb Korma
Bengan Ka Bharta
Vegetable Biriyani
Onion Kulcha
Ras Malai
Dil Bahar

Mithi Lassi
Masala Chaya

(An outdoor summer supper)

MICHELE EVANS, *Author*

Fresh Caviar with Thin Toast Points
Sauteed Soft-Shell Crabs
Fresh Asparagus with Lemon Butter
Fraises de Bois and Crème Fraiche

Champagne

or a meal prepared by a now fearless cook.

index

notes

notes

THE BEST OF THE BESTSELLERS
FROM WARNER BOOKS!

THE WOMAN'S DRESS FOR SUCCESS BOOK   (87-672, $3.95)
by John T. Molloy
The runaway bestseller by America's foremost clothing engineer which tells women who want to get ahead how to dress like a winner. "John Molloy will help put women in the boss's chair by sharing his advice on how to dress for a successful business career."—**Chicago Tribune**

SINGLE by Harriet Frank, Jr.   (81-543, $2.50)
A brilliant, moving novel about the lives, loves, tragedies and dreams of four "ordinary" women searching for happiness, finding it, losing it, crying or rejoicing over it, starting over, hanging on, making do . . . and surviving.

ANNA HASTINGS by Allen Drury   (81-603, $2.50)
With the speed of a wire service teletype, Anna Hastings shot out of the press gallery to become the founder of Washington's leading newspaper. But she paid a lifelong price for her legendary success.

SPARE PARTS by David A. Kaufelt   (81-889, $2.50)
A young reporter suddenly inherits controlling interest in a world-famous hospital. The hospital's uncanny success with transplant operations spurs the new owner's curiosity until he discovers a macabre secret entwined in a network of madness and treachery. A bizarre thriller more shocking than "Coma."

THE BONDMASTER BREED   (81-890, $2.50)
by Richard Tresillian
The dazzling conclusion to the epic of Roxborough plantation, where slaves are the prime crop and the harvest is passion and rage.

THE MINNESOTA CONNECTION   (90-024, $1.95)
by Al Palmquist with John Stone
The terrifying true story of teenage prostitution in the vicious pipeline between Minneapolis and New York, and of a tough preacher-cop's determination to break it.

THE BEST OF THE BESTSELLERS
FROM WARNER BOOKS!